THEN THE
EARTH SWALLOWED
—— THEM WHOLE ——

The Secret of Circular 3591

E.J. WADE

Then the Earth Swallowed Them Whole
The Secret of Circular 3591
By E.J. Wade

ISBN: 9798859186921

Photography by E.J. Wade

Book Design by E.J. Wade

A Novel by E.J. Wade

Library of Congress
First Edition

Table of contents

Voice over radio: SOS, SOS There is an attack on Negro residents in the area of Ocoee. Please stay clear of the Ocoee and Apopka area. SOS, may God save our souls.

New Ku Klux Klan members, who have not completed
the initiation through the gun, sword and noose. Stone
Mountain, Georgia. (The Everette Collection)

ACT One

Chapter One

EXODUS

Apopka, Florida

Gator Clouds and a few of his men drive up to a swamp area. They pull a black resident of Apopka, Florida out of the car and push him to the ground. Gator walks up to the man while he is on his knees. "I thought I told you to stop trying to get your people to vote", says Gator. The middle-aged man looks up at Gator with blood on his face. ""It is our right now, for the Negro people to vote", says the man as he tried to catch his breath. The man begins to pray. "Don't pray to God, pray to me", says Gator. "Mr. Gator, if you let me live, I will never talk about voting again. Never!" says the gentleman. "Next time, I shoot and then tell everybody we fed you to the gators, you got me boy?", asked Mr. Clouds. "Yes sir, I will never ever do it again sir", the gentleman replies. Gators men begin to grow restless. "Is it Sunday yet?" Gator asked one of the men. "We have one hour to go", says Gators driver. "On second thought, let's just get rid of him before Sunday starts", orders Gator. The man tries to beg for his life again but before he can, one of Gator's men fires his weapon.

Ocoee, Florida

July Perry is awakened by the smell of fresh breakfast cooked by Missy. She wanted to show her thanks to July Perry for hiring one of her sons to work in the orange groves. The Orange groves in Central Florida were considered gold. Julius July Perry had managed to work his way up as a labor organizer and was financially well off. Missy was waiting at the door as Estelle Perry greeted her. "Don't be a stranger, come on in", says Estelle. Missy adds her dish to the rest of the cooked food on the dinner table.

July Perry comes out his room smiling and greets Missy. "Welcome, you and your two boys are welcome here. You just make sure you save me some of that orange juice." One of Missy's sons was only 8 and too young to work but his older brother was. "Now James, my people work hard out there, and I pay them well. I expect you to work hard too", says July Perry. James shakes his head as he reaches for a muffin. "Do you know who Booker T. Washington was?", asked July Perry. James shakes his head and so does his younger brother Jimothy. "You don't know Jimothy, stop fibbing!", says James. Missy stops the two brothers from fighting. "You two hush, stop fighting in front of Mr. Perry.".

Estelle hands July Perry a newspaper. He reads it and then looks disappointed. "The Confederates and the Klan will be marching through Florida to celebrate. What are they going to celebrate? Only God knows". "Don't start being all grouchy in front of these children", says Estelle. July Perry frowns at her and then reaches for one of the muffins. "I just love your dresses", Estelle compliments Missy. Missy thanks July Perry and his wife for the meal and Mr. Perry walks them to the door. "Listen, you boys take care of your momma, any of you see any men marching through with white sheets on their heads get down and stay down until your mom tells you to come out", says July. The two young men nod their heads at Mr. Perry. "Jimothy, you're getting really tall boy, that's what I'm gonna call you from now on, Tall boy". Jimothy smiles, as he loves his new nickname. James becomes jealous and wants a name as well. "Can I have a name too Mr. Perry?" "Your name is show up to work on time", responds Mr. Perry. He laughs as he closes the door on James. As Missy and her two sons walk away,

Jimothy looks back at July Perry's house. "Mom, I want to grow up and be like Mr. Perry", says Jimothy. You're going to be plain old Jimothy", says James. Missy gives the two boys the mother stare to get them to calm down. Missy stops her two sons, lecturing them. "Do you see how well Mr. Perry treats his wife? When you grow up and have a family of your own, that's how you better treat your wife. Do you hear me boys?" Jimothy shakes his head in confusion but James understands because he is old enough to court young women.

Chicago, Illinois

Lucille had begged her mother for months to be able to meet the great Ida B. Wells. Her mother finally saved up enough to take Lucille to Chicago. Ida B. Wells had already written the Red Record and became a civil rights icon. Ida B. Wells sits before a small intimate crowd, discussing the state of America. "I knew Susan B Anthony, there were times that we agreed and there were times we're like most Americans she simply didn't get it. In America, for Afro American women, being strong is a necessity but having family was even more of a necessity. At the end of the day, when it is all said and done, if you're lucky then family will be all you have left. I have met lots of people and I have had to work with many faces but at the end of the day my family made Ida B. Wells-Barnett". The small crowd claps for miss Wells-Barnett.

After her speech, Ida B. Wells-Barnett talks with the crowd. Lucille's mother walks her up to meet miss Wells-Barnett. "Hi young lady, it is such a pleasure to meet you. I see your mom bought you here today", says Ida. "She is shy, but she begged me to meet you, this little girl would not rest until she met Ida Bell Wells, "says Nancy. Lucille manages to gather the courage to finally ask Miss Wells - Barnett a question. "What made you become a journalist? ", asked Lucille. "Well young lady, you are old enough to hear the truth. We have reached a point in America where somebody had to start telling the truth. That somebody just happened to be me. That somebody could be you." Lucille is blown away by the fact that the living legend had acknowledged her. At that moment she knew she wanted to follow the footsteps of Ida B. Wells. Ida B Wells addresses Nancy next. "Where are you guys from?" asked Ida B. Wells. "Unfortunately, we live in the South. The people aren't too friendly to our kind", Nancy replies. "Well, America is the South. You are going to meet racist people wherever you go. But I pray for a safe journey for you and your daughter", says Ida B. Wells. You could see in her eyes that she meant every word she said.

Nancy and her daughter Lucille step outside and look around at Chicago. Things appear to be getting back to normal after black residents were attacked during the Red Summer of 1919. Nancy holds her daughter's hand and worries as mob rule continues to sweep America. A young man walks by it offers Nancy a newspaper. She buys it for her daughter so that she can practice reading. The two head off to return to Ocoee, FL.

Ocoee, Florida.

July Perry and Mose Norman watch the workers work in the orange grove. The hot Florida sun beams down on them. Young adults labor in order to bring money into their families. One of the young men calls July Perry over to see something. He had found a coin on the ground. July

Perry nods for the young man to keep the money. "I need you to keep an eye on the workers, while I go see a man about a vote", says July. "You're going to see Judge Cheney aren't you?", asked Mose. "Yes, men and women should be able to vote this election. We are going to exercise our beloved right", responds Perry. July Perry did not show too much flash, he got into a normal car and was off to see judge Cheney.

July Perry arrives at judge Cheney's office. John Cheney was running for the U.S. Senate. He was temporarily appointed by Judge Taft but was not confirmed for a full term of his own by the senate. "Judge Cheney how goes it?", asked Perry. "Mr. Perry, how can I help you today?" July Perry has a seat in front of the former judge. "I am thinking about paying the poll tax for a few people, I just wanted to ask a question or two", says July Perry. "Are you familiar with judge Taft", asked Cheney. "I've heard the name", Perry replies. "Well, rumor is Taft is the next Supreme Court Chief Justice", says Cheney. "Is that good news or bad news?", asked Perry. "Well, let's just say he was not a big fan of all of the killing last year", says Cheney. What was your question, Mr. Perry. "What if they decide to lock us up for voting, how do we get out?", asked July. "If they lock you up for voting, they will be in violation of the law", responds Cheney. "Mr. Cheney, forgive me if I don't have that much faith in our justice system, but they could get it wrong", says July. "Mr. Perry, United States V. Cruikshank is starting to be frowned upon. The madness can't last forever", says John Cheney. July Perry stands and gets ready to leave. "You know Mr. Cheney, you would think a bunch of graduates of fancy ass schools like Harvard and Yale would get the 14th amendment correct. But what do I know, I'm just a Negro".

July Perry returns to see the workers off and speak to Norman. "Did the judge say anything good", asked Mose Norman. "He says we shouldn't have a problem voting and I can pay a few people's poll taxes if I want. "July, if word get out, that you're paying poll taxes for Negroes, those white folks gonna hang you from a tree", says Mose. "We don't have to bring attention to ourselves, let's just get it done", responds July Perry. July Perry continues, "besides, if they pull a gun on me, they better kill me, because I'm holding court my damn self. I ain't waiting on no jury to decide If they were wrong. I would already be hanging from a tree by then. A black man can't get no justice in America, especially not Florida. "Are we voting?", asked Mose. "Negroes are going to vote. In this election, we will vote", says Perry.

Tall Boy is running around playing in the front yard with other children. A few of the children laugh at his pants because his legs are too long for them. Tall Boy looks at the children confused. "Your pants are short", says Lucille. "My mom said I grow faster than weeds", says Jimothy. Missy comes out to check on the children. A young white male was watching. He walks up to meet Missy at her front door. "May I help you Mr. Salisbury?", asked Missy. "I was looking for your brother", says Sam Salisbury. "Well, he doesn't live here, I don't know where he lays his head" says Missy. "Well, have you heard anything about July Perry paying your brothers poll tax so that he can vote?" asked Mr. Salisbury. "I am afraid not sir", says Missy. Sam Salisbury looks around the yard one last time. He looks at Missy with anger in his eyes and then leaves.

July Perry gathers his daughter Coretha and his wife Estelle. He had a total of 6 children. Coretha, Louise, Mack, Clifford, Charlie and Betsy Perry. "Listen, if you ever hear some gunshots, or hear me say towards the moonlight, don't ask any questions, just gather each other and run". Coretha shakes her head. "Coretha, you know how to shoot, if you can get to a gun, and you have to shoot your way out, then do it", says July Perry. "Is everything alright father?", asked Coretha. "We believe in God sweety, everything is always going to be alright", he responds.

The following day July Perry meets in front of Ocoee Masonic Lodge number 66. He meets Vincent Hightower, one of his friends. "I heard you were busy getting people registered to vote", says Hightower. "Brother how has your family been?", asked July Perry. "My family is a praying family good sir", says Hightower. Mr. Hightower continues, "I heard you made Bluford Sims and some white folks angry". Mr. Perry thinks for a second. "Negroes are going to vote. We're not taking no for an answer. I'm going to stand up for what's right and I'm going to make them follow the law!", proclaims July Perry. Vincent Hightower looks him in the eye. "Make them follow the law?", he asked. The two men shake hands. July Perry hands Hightower a letter before walking into a dining hall next to the lodge. A table full of men stand up to greet July Perry. The dining hall is decorated, and everything is blue, white and gold. As the group of men are served dinner, a brother stands up and gives a toast to July Perry. "I just want to say that our Senior Warden has taken the time out of his busy life to get involved in this community and we love him for it", says the brother. The men raise their glasses and chant to July Perry.

A few men gather at an election polling place prior to election day. One of the workers' named Author speaks to Sam Salisbury. "What should we do if the niggers try to vote. I hear they're going to make some kind of ruckus", says Author. "If they show up, suggest to them that they leave. If they give you "sass", then someone will see them. Let them know we make house calls", says Salisbury. "I hope none of these boys are stupid enough to show up, trying to vote", says Author. Sam Salisbury doesn't look worried. "I'm counting on it", he says. His men left, while he decided to stay and look around the neighborhood. It was beautiful land and you could hear and feel the nature.

November 2, 1920

July Perry sits at his table and eats breakfast with his wife Estelle. She looks nervous as she hands July Perry the newspaper, Election Day was upon them. He reaches out and touches his wife's hand then assures her that everything will be alright.

Mose Shows up at the election poll without July Perry and attempts to vote. Author, one of the poll workers, meet Mose at the door with a threatening look. "You know your kind isn't supposed to be voting, just what do you think you're doing?", asked Author. Mose replies, "Well this is a free country and according to the law I can vote, so just let me through so that I can vote." Two other men show up at their door to back Author. One of the men raised their voice. "Stop being a troublemaker and get out of here Moses. "Listen, we don't want to have to use our guns but, we got plenty of them boy", says Author. Mose Turns and begins to walk away, he turns back to say something. "I'm not afraid of your guns, I guarantee I vote today. "What did you just say boy?", says author. He looks at the other two men in disbelief. That boy just threatened me. He has a gun." The other two men looked confused because they didn't see a gun. "Raise Salisbury, tell him we got an insurrection on our hands", says Author. One of the men leaves to go get Sam Salisbury. Mose heads in the direction of July Perry's house.

Mose arrives at the home of July Perry and knocks on the door. July Perry comes to the door in a hurry. "I'm gonna pack my stuff and leave I just wanted to stop and say goodbye, they're not gonna let me vote and now they're putting a price on my head for trying. I'm just tired of evil", says Mose. July Perry pauses before responding. "You already tried to vote? I thought I said something about all of us voting together", Says Perry. "John Cheney Is going to fix the problem, just go talk to him first. But for me, I think it's over", says Mose. "Why don't you stay, and we fix this together. We can both go to Cheney", says July. Mose grows angry. "No, I'm leaving the South. I'm tired of begging these crackers for rights that are already mine. I'm tired of the government being a part of it, everybody playing stupid. I'm done brother." The two men shake hands and then Mose heads to his home to gather a few things before leaving.

Sam Salisbury gathers at an office Starts to deputize men from the neighborhood. He hands them guns from a storage locker. "I have been waiting for this day for a long time said Sam, time to get rid of our nigger problem." They sit patiently and wait for the other men to show up.

Sam Salisbury shows up at the home of July Perry, with three men, they were all armed. Salisbury tries to open the door and then knocks on it hard as he can. "Come on out boy, we just want to talk to you", says Sam. On the other side of the door, July Perry hands one of his guns to his daughter Coretha, who was trained to shoot. "Hey, maybe you could come back later, and we can sort this all out, I have kids in here", Says July Perry. "Well, you and your troublemaker friend started it and I'm here to finish it. Where is that troublemaker Norman? I know you're hiding him July", says Sam. Perry replies, "Mose isn't here, he left Ocoee already, Now stop this madness and leave my home, you're scaring my kids".

Sam Salisbury signals for one of the men to sneak around the back and try to enter the home. The man kicks open the door and runs into the home with July Perry. He heads straight to July and strikes him in the head. The two men start to tussle. Sam Salisbury and the other two men head towards the back as well.

The scene goes pitch black and you can hear gun shots…

A Doctor tends to the arm of Sam Salisbury, who was struck by a bullet. He yells as he bleeds all over the Doctors coat. A man named Scott comes to check up on Sam Salisbury. "Has the war begun brother?", asked Scott. Sam Salisbury breathes hard and looks over at Scott. "Start with Perry", he says.

Back at the home of July Perry, while they are gathering their things, A mob of Ku Klux Klan members show up and begin shooting at the home. Coretha Is getting her siblings ready when a bullet strikes her in the arm. The man continued to fire at the house. July Perry looks outside and sees over a dozen men. "We can't win this gunfight. You need to get your mom and brothers to safety. Can you do that for me?", asked July. Coretha presses a clothe against her gun shot and shakes her head. Estelle tries to get to July, but the bullets come flying into the home. "She yells I love you as July Perrys family escape through a side window and leave.

Scott tells the men to cease fire. "Perry, surrender now, or we will burn your house down with your family in it". July Perry opens the front door and tosses his gun. "I'm coming out, don't shoot", he says. The men take Perry into custody. One of the men looks around the home and comes out to report that the family was gone. "Time to answer for your crimes Perry", says Scott. "They came into my home", says July. One of the men hits him and they shove him into a car. Frank Gordon tells Perry to shut his mouth and wait for justice before closing the door on him.

The Klansman begin to ride through the black populated area of Ocoee. They start to shoot at any black residents they see. A group of Klansman show up to Ocoee Lodge 66. They get ready to take a torch to it. Author runs over. "Wait, not the Masonic Lodge!", he shouts. The Klan member looks back at him. "Were not praying in the black man's temple. Burn it to the ground, he says. Ocoee is now all white. The Klansman ran inside the lodge and desecrated it, then they set fire to it.

A young Allen Franks home was attacked while trying to sleep. Mr. Franks has to grab his brother, who can't walk and carry him out on his on back as the Klan shoot at the home. The little kids duck and run towards the swampy area as the KKK shoots at little children. Next the Klan heads over to the Hightower home and fire at the windows but the residents had already gotten word and taken off. A neighbor steps outside and yells "hey, you can't do that. The Klansmen turn and fire on the man, killing him instantly.

The Klan show up at Lucille's home. Her mother grabs a gun that belonged to her late husband. "Lucille, we have to make a run for it", her mother says. "But this is our home replies Lucille". Her mother grabs a coat for her. "Listen, we have no time to argue, get your shit and let's go!", her mom says. Nancy looks out her window and sees a Klans man approaching the door. "Are you ready baby" she whispers. Young Lucille nods her head. Nancy, who had put on a pair of her late husbands' boots kicked the door hitting the Klan member and making him fall to the ground. She grabs Lucille by the hand, and they head towards the swampy area. "Don't look back baby" she says. Lucille drops a doll and tries to go back for it, but her mother stops her. They look up and see the Klan member fresh on their tale. Nancy draws the gun and opens fire at the Klan member 3 times. He turns and runs in the other direction. They turn and continue to run.

Tall Boy and his mother hear all of the shooting. Missy tells the kids to get down and stay down. She peaks out of the window and sees a Klansman staring back at her. Missy is so startled that she falls to the ground. She could hear him outside telling others that someone was home. A few other men show up and they attempt to break down Missy's front door. She places her back against the door and tries to keep the men out. One of the men takes a step back and then shoots through the door, striking Missy a few times. The last thing she sees is her youngest son Jimothy in a corner hiding.

Jimothy, who was frozen by the gunshots is grabbed by his older brother James and they make their way out of the back door. As they head towards the swampy area with no belongings a few Klansman spot the two boys. The Klan member fires a few shots. Both young men fall to the ground. The Klansman approaches to see if they were both dead. He sees no movement and then signals back to the other men. The men walk away laughing with joy and glee. Jimothy plays dead until he can't hear anyone around, then he pushed the lifeless body of his older brother James off him. Jimothy runs away through the alligator infested swamp as a gator chumps at him. He keeps running until he can see a road leading out of Ocoee.

The white mob begins to go through the homes of the black residents. They begin to loot them and take the belongings and valuables out. Author sees someone checking on the Hightower home, it is a black man. He yells hey, so the man takes off running. Author doesn't give chase. One of the Klan members shows up and takes off his hood. "Did you see one?" he asked. Author says no, he had seen enough killing for one day. Over 30 black men, women and children had been shot or beaten to death. A price to be paid for the sin of attempting to vote. The Klan members begin removing their hoods and shaking hands with each other. Some of the men go back and check on Sam Salisbury and his wounded arm. "Did we get them all?" asked Sam. "No, niggers run too fast to get them all", says one of the Klan members. "Sam greets the other members who come walking into the office. "Come tomorrow, Ocoee will be for white folks only. We don't need anymore criminals in our town", says Salisbury.

The next morning there is a mass exodus of any black person living within the Ocoee town limits. They are told to grab what they can carry and to never return. The white residents and local government take the homes of hundreds of black residents and auction them off for a nickel. Captain Bluford Sims approaches Sam Salisbury. "I want July Perrys house", he says. Salisbury nods and points at the house of July Perry. The crown jewel of the black community. Sims flips a coin over to one of the politicians and then takes possession of July Perrys home.

Judge Cheney steps out of his home in Orlando, Florida. He sees the dead body of Julius July Perry hanging. There was a sign on him that read "no more voting". Judge Cheney decides he had seen enough and decides to leave the Orlando area. Mose Norman had made it out and fled to New York, never to return.

The Ku Klux Klan at their height in the 1920's
(The Everette Collection)

Gator Clouds arrives in Apopka, Florida. He meets in a former Hall of the White League, now owned by the Ku Klux Klan. Several members are meeting on the inside and bragging about what happened in Ocoee. "You should have seen it, Gator", says Author. "The niggers had it coming to them. I'm proud of you boys. Damn proud. Sam didn't flinch. Good man. I'm tired of these animals trying to take the white man's country. It's about time Florida joined the rest of the fight against tyranny", says Gator. Gator shares his whiskey flask with others in celebration. "I want to be like those brave men in Ocoee when I grow up", jokes Gator Clouds.

The following day, the newspapers only mentioned two white men killed in Ocoee. It didn't mention the 30 plus black victims of the massacre, or the land grab and mass exodus of residents. While there were investigations and reporting by organizations like the NAACP, the white residents of Ocoee agreed that the event didn't happen. The government agreed that no rights were violated, in agreement with United States V. Cruikshank.

Chapter Two

SMEARED ON THE WALL

Moore V. Dempsey

Moore et. Al. V. Dempsey

261 U.S. 86 (1923) No. 199

Argued January 9, 1923

Chief Justice William Howard Taft

Chief Justice Taft and the other Supreme Court Justices hold their conference after hearing the oral arguments for Moore V. Dempsey. Chief Taft appointed Judge Cheney, who had witnessed the aftermath of the Ocoee Massacre. He was fed up with Federal Courts not doing their job. The men shake hands and have a seat. "Giving the evidence made in the oral arguments, I don't see how one could say that Elaine 12 received a fair trial. Once these racialized mobs step foot in the courtroom, they destroy Article 3 of the U.S. Constitution. The judge and jury decide the outcome, not armed, violent mobs", says Justice Taft. Justice Sutherland responds. "Chief Justice, we must be careful here. We could set a precedent where anyone can say their rights were violated and it becomes an obstacle to serving justice". Justice Taft fires back. "I am a former President of these United States, I don't need precedent explained to me, but what no one can explain is how hundreds of black citizens keep showing up dead, some shot in the back and thousands of bodies later, no one uses God given sense to say there was no due process. The 14th Amendment is a valid amendment, yes?" Justice Sutherland becomes visibly upset.

Justice Oliver Holmes speaks. "We can set a precedent of following the 14th Amendment and its intended purpose, which is equal protection under the law for Freedmen and their descendants. There are reports of U.S. Army soldiers killing negroes and the son of one of the attorneys was almost attacked by a mob. We either have a constitution or we don't". Justice Reynolds sides with Geroge Sutherland in descent. "How long are we going to let these people play victim", he says. Chief justice Taft counts the votes in a no-nonsense fashion, he was a man with a large 300 plus pound frame. He was also very intelligent and a graduate of Yale University. "6-2" he says. 6-2 is good enough. We find that the presence of a mob prevented a fair hearing. The lower court discharged their duties in a perfunctory manner. They can either cross their T's or send the men home."

Apopka, Florida.

Gator gets a newspaper with the decision from Moore V. Dempsey on the front page. He puts on his reading glasses to get a better look. Gator throws the newspaper down in anger." They're siding with the niggers", he says. "What does it mean, says one of his men as he picks his nose. "It means they just made it harder to police these animals. I knew we couldn't rely on these judges", says Gator. The person who delivers the paper gets ready to walk off, but first, he turns and says, "I just thought you should know". Gator thinks for a moment. "It had to be Tulsa or maybe some of the Army Soldiers from Arkansas went soft on us". He stands in anger and exits the porch.

Washington D.C.

Reporters rush the steps of the courthouse as Chief Justice Taft is escorted to his car by security. Someone opens the door for him, and he gets Inside. The driver pulls off. "You must have had a big case today Justice Taft", says the driver. "It's the Supreme Court, every case is a big case", he responds. Taft attends a gathering of other political and legal minds who attended Yale. One of the men approach him and shake his hand. "I know you hate politics but…" Chief Justice Taft interrupts. "Let's not talk about politics tonight". His friend smiles. "Well, some progressives may hate you, but you reshaped the Supreme Court in your image friend", he says. "It was a broken system, no matter which side of the aisle", says Justice Taft. A woman joins in on the conversation. "Chief Justice, what do you think people will say about this case 100 years from now. "I think they will say nothing", he says. "You are the man who put an end to mob rule", says his male colleague. Justice Taft pauses for a moment. "Mobs have no place in the courthouse", he says.

Jacksonville, Florida

Jimothy was taken in by his aunt and uncle in North Florida. He was filled with rage as a little boy who had lost his mother and brother. His aunt brings a meal to the table. "Make sure you pray over your food Jimothy". Jimothy pushed the bowl to the side. "Pray to who, God who let them kill my family?". His aunt slaps him in the mouth. Don't you dare commit sin in this house again. You will not grow up to feel sorry for yourself, do you hear me?", she asked. His uncle walks over and places a calm hand on his shoulder. "Tall Boy, we don't understand God, but everything in this world happens for a reason", he says. Jimothy eats his food in silence with anger brewing. His uncle walks back over to his chair. Jimothy raises his voice in anger. "Well, I'm going to get big and strong and kill them. Every one of them that touched my family". He gets up from the table and runs off. His aunt tries to follow him, but his uncle stops her. They both look sad as heartbroken Jimothy runs away.

March 8, 1930

Chief Justice William Howard Taft passes away from health complications related to weight at age 72. Moore V. Dempsey is forgotten by the general public but continues to be used as precedent. The mob violence was slowed down to a crawl and the tactics shifted to police brutality and segregation.

March 25, 1931

Lucille is attending college at Edward Waters when she gets news that the legend Ida B. Wells passed away on the radio. She breaks down crying in her dorm room. She looks outside of her dorm room. The other young ladies looked out to see what the commotion was. "She's gone, she died", says Lucille. The dorm director comes out to check on the young women. She gives Lucille a hug. "Are you ready to step up", she asked. Lucille shakes her head as the tears continue to flow.

The Dorm Director speaks to the women, who are visibly upset about the death of Ida B. Wells. "We are not going to mourn, but instead celebrate the life of Ida Bell Wells. It is up to you young ladies to step up now! It is time for you to forge your own path and turn America into a democracy. In the end, she had family and that's what we are. When the whole world let her down, she could rely on her family. And when we get to eternity, let us be able to look our sister in the face and say "I too fought evil and made the world a better place". The young women standing in the hall cheer. Ida Ida Ida Ida.

Lucille goes back into her dorm room. She looks out the window at people talking to each other outside. She was very smart but hated small talk. She begins to work on a project but has writers block, so she balls the paper up and throws it.

Lucille steps outside to get some fresh air. A young man walks by and stops to court Lucille. "Hi, where are you going looking like a princess?", the man asked. "Are you a student here, I know some of the boys aren't students here", she says. Before the young man could answer, she hit him with three more questions. "What is your intent with me? Do you want to get married one day? "Do you get good grades?", she asked. The young boy becomes intimidated and walks off saying, "never mind, weird girl". "I heard that, I didn't find it charming or witty", she yells as she fixes her glasses.

Lucille walks over to a nearby lake. "Maybe I should just jump in and drown", she says to herself. She has a flashback of the gators in the water as she fled Ocoee as a child and jumps. One of her favorite professors walks by. "Are you alright Lucille?", he asked. She is silent. "Do you think a woman should seek protection as the number 1 indicator in mating?", she asked. The professor is taken back. Well, women often gravitate towards men who can provide some type of benefit. He could be a genius in his own way or protect them in other ways. Keep focusing on the brilliant work you're doing, and you will write your own ticket anyway", says the professor. "I'm just looking toward the future, I'm not interested in any of these men in particular", she says. The professor looks at her face to gage her mood. "You're asking questions, which is what young people do.

It's when you stop asking questions that becomes a problem".

Chapter Three

NEW HEROES NEW JOURNEY

Jacksonville, Florida

Jimothy, who was now an adult, met a woman at a get together in Jacksonville, Florida. He enters an establishment that is owned by a local gangster he knew. He approaches one of the women who had just finished dancing. "Do you dance stranger?" she asked. "Not often, but if you ask nicely, I may cut a rug", says Jimothy.

The two exited the home and Jimothy walked the young lady to her home. Once inside, he looks around and discovers the woman is "well to do". "What do you do for a living? You're living high on the hog for someone who made it through the Great Depression", says Jimothy. The woman slips off her dress and reveals her incredibly in shape body. "My daddy invented things", she responded. "That's nice, we had a decent house growing up, but…" Jimothy pauses. "But what", she says. Not wanting to talk about the massacre, Jimothy chooses to hug her instead. "You don't seem like the getting hitched type of man", says the woman. "Right now, I travel the world and report stories. As soon as I find the right story, I know a newspaper down south that will take me on". The woman rubs on Jimothy and then says, "tomorrow morning, I expect you to be gone, is that ok?" she says. Jimothy nods and then turns off the light.

Ocoee, Florida

Regan prepares breakfast for her children before seeing them off to the schoolhouse. Tim is running around the dinner table irritating his older sister Rebecca. "Little boy, if you don't sit your narrow tail down, I will hit you with this bread", says Regan. "Mom, mom, mom…", Tim repeats until she answers. "The children at school said we took our house from niggers". Regan grabs Tim and makes him sit down. "That is a lie from hell and tell those kids to mind their business. We worked hard for our house just like every other good Christian white family in this town. Certain groups just want to sit around and feel sorry for themselves", says Regan. Rebecca is slow to speak. Mom, if we did take it, could we just give it back?", she says. "Their kind isn't allowed in Ocoee, and this is our home. Now eat your breakfast in silence. Have some dignity. "The Tomilson's have a colored maid. I saw her one day", says Tim. "Well, she better have her black ass out of here when that sun goes down", says Regan.

Regans husband and the children's father came downstairs. "Why are you so loud in the morning", says Wallace. "The children at school said we took this house from a nigger family", says Tim. "Eat your breakfast and listen to your mother, before I spank your hind parts" says Wallace. "This family is violent", says Tim as he finishes eating.

Regan walks her children to school. They take in the beautiful town of Ocoee. Only a few black people were allowed to work there, but they had to leave before the evening. They would clean the houses, many of them formerly owned by black residents. They drop the youngest off first and then Regan pulls her daughter to the side. "Don't forget, you have a ceremony tonight. You are 16 now, which means you're a woman.

After Regan drops off the children, she sees a black man leaving after dropping off a package to a store. "What are you doing here boy!", she yells. Regan runs over to the man. He looks down at the floor, knowing that looking directly at a white woman could get him killed. "I was just dropping something off to Mr. Lester", he says. "Well, it seems like you dropped it off, now get out of our town. Don't come back around here trying to rape our women. Do you hear me boy?" says Regan. The man shakes his head and runs away. Regan smiles with satisfaction. She enters the home and uncorks some wine and stands in the kitchen drinking it. "It's kind of early to drink", says Wallace as he reads his newspaper. Today is the day our girl finds out what monsters we are", continues Wallace. Regan pours more wine. "You provide a good life for us because my family helped pave the way. They built this town, noose by noose, so before you get on your high horse, remember that", she says to Wallace.

Orlando, Florida

Lucille landed a job at a small struggling newspaper in the Orlando area. She approaches her boss about covering events at the Whitehouse. She peeks into his office. "Hey, Grease, what did you think about my article on Chief Justice Taft?", she asked. "You could only get a quote from the security staff? "You couldn't shake the tree for nothing better?", he asked. Lucille gets offended. "Well, the Orlando Sentinel was more welcome up in D.C. than us", she fires back. "The Orlando Miracle is owned by colored folks, and we got colored folks' money. You did a good job with the analysis. Where are you living nowadays Lucille?" asked Grease. "I am in Parramore", she says. "A lot of our people leaving for the North, our money is drying up", says Grease as he hands Lucille her small check and she leaves.

Remy and Jimothy wait on the outskirts of Ocoee. A place they both once called home. "You must be crazy if you think we can just drive into Ocoee and come out alive", says Jimothy. "Tall Boy, its ok, I got uniforms for us. We can say we are there to pick up Mr. Eddie and drive him around" says Remy. Jimothy looks nervous. "Who is Mr. Eddie Negro?", asked Jimothy. Remy hands him a drivers hat to go with his uniform. "There is no Mr. Eddie, I just want to see what it looks like now", says Remy. Jimothy responds, "this Negro about to get us hung because he home sick". Remy let out a laugh, but Jimothy was obviously afraid.

The two men make there way towards Ocoee and into the neighborhood. They are spotted by residents who look at them in anger. Little white children, who were playing in their yard stop and look at the car with the two black men driving through. The men spot Jimothy's old home. "My mom and brother use to sit right there and talk while she peeled our oranges", says Jimothy. "Man, this is your house, and some white folks took it, and they burned my house to the ground", says Remy. Regan looks out the window and spot the men pulling off. She peeks her head out the door to frown at them. As the black car drives away, two cars cut the men off. One of the cars lets down its window and a man aims a gun at the two men. A large man steps out of the other car. Gator Clouds walks over to the car to meet the two black men. "Are you boys lost or something?", he says while trying to open their door handle. "Sir, we are drivers for Mr. Eddie, we just got lost", says Remy. One of Gators men opens the passenger side door and pulls Jimothy out. Gator finally gets the door open on the driver side and pulls Remy out. "We got one Ed and he would never let your kind drive him around or around his wife. You got a few seconds to explain yourself to me or catch a bullet", says Gator as he pulls a gun out. "Jimothy tries to speak but he was hit by the other man. Gator puts the gun to Remy's head.

Orlando, Florida

Lucille looks around her little home In Parramore as she thinks about accepting a job offer in Chicago. She looks down at one of her outstanding writer awards from Edward Waters College. One of her friends came knocking at her door. "Debra, hey girl, I was just thinking about asking you if you wanted to get some food", says Lucille. "You know I want some food. I came to be nosey and see if you are going to take that job up North", says Debra. "The money is better", Lucille answers. Debra looks disappointed, but hugs Lucille. "I guess you really are following in the footsteps of Ida B. Wells.

The women walk up the road to a local sandwich shop. They preferred to go to the black-owned one, so that they did not have to get served at the back of the store. The two eat their meal in silence, until Debra sees the sad look on Lucille's face. "What's wrong dear?", Debra asked. "I thought I would have a husband and children by now. It hasn't happened to me. I don't match with anybody", says Lucille with disappointment. "I keep telling you to go out into the world. You can't write all day every day. The love of your life is out there", says Debra. "Chicago?" asked Lucille. "It's a big city, with big city people", Debra assures her.

Regan steps outside and sees Gator and his men with their guns out. "Stop, my little boy is coming home soon. I don't want him to see this!", she yells. Gator yells back, "let that boy see how to be a man. How to protect his community from rapist niggers". Regan approaches the men. "What the hell kind of uncle are you?", not in front of kids. Gator looks around and sees a few children coming home from the schoolhouse. He and his men lower their weapons. "My sister just saved your life, now get the hell out of here and don't let the Moon light catch you or we won't be so forgiving boys", says Gator. The two men get ready to get back in the car. Before they do, Jimothy looks up at his old home. "Go on now, get!", yells Regan. The two men drive off. Gator puts his hand on his sister's shoulder. "What did I tell you about correcting me in front of people?", says Gator. "What was that colored fella staring at?", asked one of Gators men. Gator just looks at the man and then gets in his car and drives off.

The two men drive back towards Apopka together. Jimothy finally breaks his silence. "That was a bad plan man. We could have gotten strung up in a tree". "They took our homes. They took our families homes. I know you're a man of peace, but there comes a time when we will have to stand up and fight brother", responds Regan. Jimothy looks out the window at the country road. "My mom used to cook for me and my older brother. She hated it when we would eat other people cooking, except that time we went to July Perry's house. She looked happy man. She looked happy and then they shot her". Remy grows even more frustrated. "If we can't be free in America, then let's just burn it down.

The entire thing. Let's make them feel our pain", he says. "You want to be like them? I guess you think women and children should die, like them too?", asked Jimothy. "Remy looks at Jimothy out of the corner of his eye. "You just don't get it, do you? They attacked us first. Slavery been over, why won't they just leave us be?"

Back in Ocoee, the "daughters of Ocoee "are invited to a celebration. Rebecca is among the young ladies; she had just turned 16 years old. A gentleman in a hat introduces himself as Mr. Upshaw. He signaled for servants to bring the young women their favorite meals. The aroma filled the dining room. Mr. Upshaw sits a top hat on top of the dinner room table. The young ladies stare at it in confusion. "It's a hat", says Amy in confusion. Mr. Upshaw smirks. "Yes, this is a hat. This is not just any hat", says Mr. Upshaw. "Is it a magic hat?" asked Amy with sarcasm. This was taken from Ocoee Lodge 66, Prince Hall. "The old men?", says Amy. Mr. Upshaw passed it around so that the young women could look at it. Rebecca refuses to touch it. "You took it from the colored people", she says. Mr. Upshaw points at her. "We protected Ocoee by driving out an evil race of criminal, savage people. If they would have stayed in Ocoee, they would rape and kill every one of you!" The room of young women gasp. Mr. Upshaw continues, "We rescued Ocoee from evil people, and they sold us these houses. "Who are they?", asked Rebecca. "The township, fair and square. They rewarded us with this land and property, and I am sure the blacks got compensated. Now, we keep them out, to keep you safe. I believe you owe us a debt of gratitude. I tell you this, because one day they will return. That is why we keep a watchful eye over Ocoee. Rebecca heard enough, she stops eating and walks outside.

Wallace goes to check on his daughter. "Dry those eyes now", he says. "I hate this world dad, why are people so mean and hateful?" "I suppose they figure they are protecting the white race. "From what?", asked Rebecca. He rubs her back. "Whoever tries to harm us, I guess". She looks at her father with tears flowing from her eyes. "What do you believe, dad?", she asked. "I believe whatever your mom tells me to", he responds. "Then you're a coward dad. A coward", she responds in disappointment. He continues to rub her back for support. "That's it, take it all out on your poppa. But remember this, the family that listens to each other, always stays together". Rebecca dries her eyes and gives her father a hug. "Timmy knows", the kids at school told him. Wait, is our house really stolen?" Wallace is silent. Rebecca runs off towards their home before he could respond. He gets ready to run after her but is stopped by Mr. Upshaw. "Your little girl has nigger lover in her blood. I see where she gets it from", says Mr. Upshaw. Wallace gives him a hard push. "Wait until Gator hears about this", says Upshaw. Wallace smirks. "Go right ahead, she is his only niece. He will turn you into gator bait", says Wallace as he walks off.

Rebecca busted through the door back at home to confront her mother. Regan was already at the table drinking whiskey from a flask. "Well, the truth is out", she says. Rebecca slaps her mother's drink out of her hand. She leans over and gets in her mom's face. "You claim to be some Christian. You took everything from the colored people!" Regan stands up calmly and then proceeds to slap the shit out of Rebecca. "You little ungrateful bitch. Who do you think you're talking to?" Rebecca picks herself up off the ground. Her mother continues, "I provide for you and give you everything. Your bloomers, your food, your hair cut! You little bitch, I made you. I brought you into this world and I can take you out". She walks circles around her daughter. "Now you know who is in charge and you will shut your mouth and follow my leadership, or your uncle is going to fix you!" Rebecca stands tall with tears falling from her eyes. "Someday a handsome man is going to take you away from here. It will be because I made you into a good woman". She walks off and leaves Rebecca stunned with tears in her eyes.

Chicago, Illinois

Lucille writes home:

Chicago is colder than I thought but I like it here. You can find some degree of peace away from the rule of white mobs and Klansman. I am working for a larger paper and hope to have my own paper someday. I must admit, I feel alone at times. I know God has plans for me. We all have a purpose in life, I think I am serving mine, at lease at the surface. I don't know what the future holds for America, but I do know that we are made in the image of God, and they can't hold us back for long.

Washington, D.C.

An assistant rush through the hall to try to get to President Franklin D. Roosevelts office as quick as possible. People move out of the way, as the man moves fast as if his job depended on it. The young man burst into the President's office. "Excuse me fellas, my young assistant seems to be lost", says President Roosevelt as everyone laughs. "Well lad, spit it out already". A. Phillip Randolph, he met with the First Lady Sir. The Negroes are going to march on Washington. They're saying we can't spread democracy all over the world and not have democracy here". President Roosevelt drops his smile. "Get me Philip Randolph on the phone, now. How does a bunch of union members get that kind of power", says President Roosevelt.

June 25th 1941

President Roosevelt gathers the White House Press to make an announcement. "Today, I will sign into law, Executive Order 8802. As we prepare to aide the allied forces in spreading democracy all over the world, we can't be hypocrites and deny our Negro citizens the right to fair labor practices. We are banning unfair labor practices in the Federal Government and when dealing with the defense industry. We are also going to establish a Fair Employment Practices Commission. Everyone in America, regardless of skin color, should have the opportunity to feed their families". President Roosevelt signs the Executive Order and then leaves the press area.

ACT *Two*

Chapter four

SKY FIRE

December 7, 1941

Lucille walks into a small Theatre, where the black people had to sit in the top and white people sat on the bottom. A special announcement comes on the screen. Japan had just attacked and destroyed most of the Naval Fleet at Pearl Harbor. The footage shows smoke clouds all over the screen at Pearl Harbor. Lucille and the other black people look on in horror as the white audience grows angry. Finally, a man yells "The Japs and the evil Axis must be stopped". Another man screams "Death to the Japs". The black people begin to leave the theatre in fear of being attacked they walk home. A fellow reporter walks with Lucille. "They said a Negro man named Doris Miller fought back. He manned a gun and shot back at the pilots". Lucille has a moment of silence. "Well if America is going to war, and I think we are, then I should go report on him and any other service men who would be willing to talk to me", says Lucille. She takes off running and then runs back to hug her friend. "Be safe, we are going to war", her friend says. Lucille runs off and tries to see if she could get on the military base to meet Doris Miller.

The Secret of World War 2
Circular 3591, December 12, 1941

President Franklin Roosevelt calls U.S. Attorney Francis Biddle into his office. His secretary brings him some water as he looks around the legendary office. "Let's have a look at what you came up with, says the President. President Roosevelt looks at the memo. "Are you telling me we still have slaves in the United States?!", he says. "Mr. President, whenever we try to take someone to court for one of these peonage cases, they claim there is no debt. The poor blacks may just be selling themselves to a white person". FDR looks up to the attorney. "Who in the world would believe that thousands of black people are selling themselves to whites and there is no debt!?" These are very hard cases to prove", says the attorney. "We are feeding the Japanese propaganda machine by having anything that looks like slavery. You need to adjust your wording, accordingly, quietly put out Circular 3591 and lock up a few white people". The U.S. Attorney stands up and says, "right away Mr. President". President Roosevelt throws the draft of the memo on the table. "Modern day slavery. The communist would ruin us!", he says.

Beeville, Texas

The U.S. Attorney sends Marshals to Mr. Skrobarcck's home in Texas to arrest him and his 29-year-old daughter. "The U.S. Attorney shows him his badge. "You both are under arrest for the crime of slavery in the U.S.. "Wait, I'm white and he's colored", says Mr. Skrobarcck. "Why does that matter, a crime is a crime. "Please don't arrest my daughter, this is our way of life down here. We ain't harm nobody", he says. The Marshals handcuff Mr. Skrobarcck and his daughter. Other officers go into the home and the outhouse on the side and look around. They bring out Alfred Irving, the last American slave. One of the officers help him walk, he had been beaten until he was crippled. Neighbors gather around to watch. One of the men yell, "that ain't right, coming in here arresting a white man over a nigger". One of the officers walks over to the man. "We can't rescue the world from bondage if we have it here". The Feds drive off with Mr. Skrobarcck and his daughter as the neighbors grow angry. "the elite Yankees keep taking our property and bringing tyranny to the south!", a man yells.

Jacksonville, Florida

Remy and Jimothy find themselves being drafted for the U.S. Army. They line up at a Military Processing Station. A Army Seargent announces Jimothy's full name, Jimothy Williams. It was the first time being called by his full name by a white person, he was startled. "Step forward now!", says the Officer. Jimothy steps forward. "Are you ready to go serve your country and fight for America?", asked the officer. "I don't mind defending America, but we, the negro people should enjoy the same rights as you sir. "Get over it, this war is bigger than race", says the officer. Remy is called by his full name, Charles Manning the 2nd. Jimothy smirks when he hears Remy's name. Remy frowns at him. "I'm ready to go fight", says Remy. "Negroes will mostly be in support roles. The Generals don't have confidence in your ability to fight side by side with white soldiers. You may get them killed", says the officer. The two men are handed orders and they leave.

Pearl Harbor

A few reporters were able to speak with Doris Miller. He was set to receive a Navy Cross for his service in combat from Admiral Nimitz. "How does a cook learn to shoot a 50 caliber anti-aircraft gun?", asked a reporter. "A lieutenant who was wounded asked me to help carry some injured shipmates to safety and then he showed me where to load it. I guess after that, I just used whatever God given sense I have. A white reporter smirks. "I am sure you were afraid. What made you risk your life?", asked another reporter. "I couldn't stop, I didn't think about the fear. I just wanted to get my shipmates out of harms way", says Miller. Doris Miller gets ready to excuse himself but makes one more comment first. "Maybe Negro men will get more opportunities in the military because we are willing to die for our country too", he says.

Doris Miller walks away but is stopped by Lucille. "I got to meet Ida B. Wells as a girl and now I get to meet a real American hero", she says. He smirks, yes ma'am, I was just doing my job", he says. "Such a humble young man. May God watch over you on your journey young man", says Lucille. He shakes her hand and gets ready to leave.

1942

A Japanese family is returning to their home from dinner. They are surprised when they are met by armed soldiers and a man in a suit and tie. Mr. Akari asked, "what is the meaning of this?", when grabbed by the arm by a soldier. "The War Relocation Authority requires that your family be moved to one of twelve zones for our protection and safety", says the gentleman in the suit. "I am Nisei, I am an American citizen. I have rights", says Mr. Akari. One of the soldiers places their hand on their side arm. "Don't worry, you will have time to pack, and we will keep you informed. You won't be in the dark", says the gentleman in the suit. "I will not be treated like a colored person!", yells Mr. Akari. The soldiers ignore him and push them into their home to start packing their belongings.

Japanese American citizens and residents, who are not citizens are being placed on buses all up and down the pacific coast. Armed soldiers are showing up and they are being handed orders to report to one of twelve zones. Mr. Akari helps his family board a train in California. He sneaks a clothe from his pocket and wipes a tear from his eye. A tear that he didn't want his family to see. "It's ok dear, we will get everything back", he says to his wife. As the train pulls away, Mr. Akari spots a white family screaming "Japs go home!" at him. The Japanese were being treated like Negroes. One of the passengers stands up and yells, "I am American!" Mr. Akari tells him to save his energy for the fight to come in their native language.

Camp Claiborne, Louisiana

Lucille steps off a bus and enters the Army base with an escort to interview the segregated soldiers. The 761st Tank Battalion. The Sergeant walks in and prepares the men. "There is a reporter here from Chicago, I just want to remind you to be on your best behavior. She is here to report on Negro soldiers serving in The War", he says. She speaks to several soldiers one by one. As one of the young men stands, he calls out "hey Tall Boy, you're next. We got a pretty reporter"! Lucille's heart skips a beat when she hears the name Tall Boy. Jimothy enters the room and squints. He turns and gets ready to walk out. "Wait! Jimothy", she says. He stops in his tracks and takes another look at the woman. "Lucille?" She walks over and hugs him.

Jimothy and Lucille have lunch together. "We get the best meals when visitors come", says Jimothy. "Why did you turn to walk away from me?", asked Lucille. "I'm not that person anymore. I don't know who I am. I don't want to be reminded of everything I lost". Lucille grows angry. "I lost stuff too", she says. "I lost my mom and brother, looks like you and yours made it out just fine!", says Jimothy. She stands and hugs Jimothy. "I'm not him anymore, I'm not him anymore", he repeats. "I know, I want to get to know you now. Whoever you are, alright?" She hugs Jimothy as he fights to hold back tears. Jimothy tries to cheer himself up. "Come here, I want to show you something", he says. He walks Lucille over to the place he goes for peace. "Nobody knows about my quiet place. I come here to think. I come here to dream about what my life could have been". Lucille walks around and looks at the green grass and the blue sky. "When this war is over you should move to Chicago", says Lucille. "I work on Tanks, what can I do in Chicago?", he asked. Lucille doesn't reply. "Besides, after this war, we are going to fight another war", says Jimothy. "What are you talking about?" she asked. "We are going to end Sundown towns in Florida. We will have freedom in Florida or Florida will burn". Lucille looks worried. "We won't get Ocoee back. It belongs to the whites now", she says. He kisses her hand. "You can be a reporter, in Chicago", says Lucille, trying to get him to change his mind. He looks at her with sorrow. "I'll more than likely die in Florida", says Jimothy.

August 6, 1945

The soldiers in the 761st Tank Battalion gather in Fort Hood, Texas. By this time, they were slightly older and more mature, and some had even seen combat after Army Generals decided to give them a chance fighting Germany. A soldier walks in the barracks and yells "Black Panthers! Come out Fighting. The men shout "come out fighting!" A sergeant walks in and tells the men to report to the war room. They put on a special presentation. Today, with the help of scientist and J. Robert Oppenheimer, two B12 bombers have dropped 2 atomic bombs on the cities of Hiroshima and Nagasaki. The death tolls have now passed 70,000 and is growing. Jimothy stands up and starts to have a panic attack. "Tall Boy", someone calls out. "Oh my God, they killed civilians, didn't they?", he asked. The sergeant approaches. "Keep your military bearing soldier. The Japs killed plenty of our men. Let's not forget who started this war!" Jimothy storms out of the hall. The sergeant yells, "we set the sky on fire!" One of the soldiers stands up. "Our boys are coming home. The Japanese ain't no friend of the Negro. The men have mixed reactions. Jimothy stands outside and imagines the sky on fire. The sergeant walks outside to find Jimothy. "Never walk away from me again. You're going to go home and marry that girl and have babies", says the sergeant. He shakes Jimothy's hand and walks away.

Gator's Dream

Gator see's African American soldiers returning after World War 2. He looks on with envy at their uniforms. A few of the men walk by one of Gator's shops happy, celebrating coming home. Gator is standing over his older brother's grave, who died in World War 1. He is a little kid, with feelings of sadness that he is not able to understand. His father is attending his brother's funeral. "Jerry, go sit down and eat and stop being a burden at your own brother's funeral", his mother says. Jerry takes off running instead of listening to his mom. His father finally catches up to him and sits him down. "Hey, with your oldest brother gone, you and Kenny are going to have to watch over the shop when you are older. "I want to fight in war too. I want to be a soldier too", says young Jerry. "Dammit boy, I don't need two sons dying in wars. Go pick up a book or something and stop making a fuss", his father says. Jerry emerges from the swamp. He wades through the water dragging a dead body out of the swampy water with him. "Look dad, I saved my brother", says Jerry. He looks down and see's the body of a young black boy that he had killed. "Whoa", he says to himself. Judge Taft points at Gator with disapproval and nods his head. "I ain't kill nobody", he says to the judge, trying to hide his bloody hands.

Jerry is standing near a tree as his father teaches him how to tie his first noose. A few of his fathers' employees stand by and hold a crying black man. "Mr. Clouds", the man calls out. Gator's father inspects his noose to make sure he did it correctly. "You're a natural kid. You're going to be just like your other brothers", says Gator's father. The men bring a step over so that they could hang the black man from the tree. Gator's father calls him over. "You're going to kick them from underneath the coon and then his neck will snap. Do you understand?", asked his father. His father forces the man on the step and the men put a noose around the man's neck. His father signals for young Gator to kick the step and send the man to his death.

Gator finds himself holding a rope. He is teaching his nephew Tim how to tie a noose. "Why do I have to learn this", says Tim. "If something happens to me, you have to protect your mother and your sister", says Gator. Tim becomes angry and throws the rope down. "I want to go play. My mom can protect herself. You see how mean she is", says Tim. "Hush, I had to protect your mom once from a wild coon", says Gator.

Regan is a younger woman. She sneaks a younger negro boy into her room. When she gets undressed, the young boy becomes afraid. He had never seen a woman in the nude before. He turns to run. Gator and his father are entering the home after hunting when they hear Regan yell "help"! The father points the gun at the young black man. "Don't you move", he says. The man stands there scared as Regan quickly puts her clothes back on. "Regan, you didn't", says her father. "No, he broke in and tried to rape me", she says. "Good, because if I ever find out you're a nigger lover, I will hang you too", her father says. Gator runs to gather a few men and then they take the young man away to kill him. The young man looks back at Regan for help, with a sad look on his face. Regan looks away from the young man.

Ida B. Wells is giving an interview to a reporter. "I said nobody in this country believes the thread-bare lie that negro men rape white women. If Southern men continue to overreach, the public will reach a conclusion that is damaging to the reputation of their women", she says. The reporter responds, "But if white men say it then it must be true". Gator yells at Ida B. Wells as she speaks to the reporter, but neither can hear him. "The white man won't stand for such evil slander", yells Gator!

Ida B. Wells continues, "If you look at the case of Ms. J.S. Underwood, the respectable preacher's wife, William Offett, served 15 years in Ohio and it was only when she got older that she felt remorse and confessed that it was not true to her husband". The reporter takes notes as Ms. Wells-Barnett speaks. Gator is pacing back and forth and yelling at Ida B. Wells as she reveals the lies that had been told that led to the lynchings of black men all over the U.S.

"There was also Sarah Clark of Memphis, who stated that she was not white in order to escape miscegenation laws and was allowed to continue her relationship with her black lover. Then there was the case of M. Strickland, the furniture salesman, who was spared a lynching after the white woman stated he was only in her room to put up curtains. These are all facts on the record", says the legendary Ida B. Wells.

Gator gets angry and throws a punch in the direction of Ida B. Wells, shattering glass and then staring at himself in a mirror. "I could have been somebody else. I could have been a soldier", says Gator to himself. He places himself at the entrance of the home where his sister told the lie of being assaulted by the young black male. He yells at his younger sister in anger. "Nigger lover!", I don't want to be part of your lies.

Gator is walking in front of an unlimited number of men. They are armed with farming tools instead of weapons. They spot a community of black farmers working. Gator yells "forward march", as the men start walking towards the farmer. Gator yells "double time", as the men speed up and charge the farmers.

Gator finds himself on a boat sailing down a river as people point to him and yell "murderer!" General Robert E. Lee waits on the riverbanks for Gator. "He could never be me", he says. Gator grows angry and tries to find a way out of the boat. "Let me out", he says. Gator begins to cry. "I hate God, why did he make them. Why couldn't the world just be white?", he asked. He hears thunder crackles from the sky.

The waters become gator infested. They chomp at the riverboat that Gator is in. A little black girl appears next to

Gator. "Will you help me", she asked. "I'll feed your little black ass to these gators you pickaninny", he says as he tries to grab the little girl, but she vanishes. Gator turns and is awaken by car headlights.

Gator wakes up at home in his bed. He shaves with a blade and then heads over to his sister's home. Gator knocks three times at the door. Regan answers. "Why are you here so early?", asked Regan. He stares at her with dead eyes but can't think of anything to say. He turns and begins to walk away. "Jerry", his sister calls him. "Are you having those nightmares again", she says. Gator nods his head. Regan hugs him and brings him into the house.

Manzanar Relocation Center, 1943, Sumiko Shigematsu
(The Everette Collection)

Paratroopers land during World War 2 near Lae, New Guinea. (The Everette Collection)

Dr. Oppenheimer and his team provide the U.S. military with the world's first Atomic Bomb (Lia Koltyrina)

Chapter Five

GATOR BAIT

Washington, D.C.

In Washington, D.C. there was a well-known lunch spot that D.C. employees eat at. A off duty officer finished his lunch and then stepped outside. He was greeted by Jimothy. "Officer Lewis, I have been looking all over for you", he says. "How do you know my name and why are you looking for me?", asked the officer. Jimothy whips out his pen and pad. "I want to ask you about Circular 3591. Did the United States government know that slavery will still going on in the United States?", he asked. The officer begins to walk off as Jimothy attempts to walk with him. "Everything is on the record, and if someone committed the crime of slavery, they were arrested", says the officer. "Why did the government allow it? "Does the 14th Amendment to the Constitution not provide equal protection under the law?", asked Jimothy. The officer walks off as Jimothy waits for an answer. "Why were there no white slaves!", he yells as the officer continues to ignore him".

Jacksonville, Florida

Lucille is with Jimothy in his small home. The second Great war had ended and the two decided to start a relationship. Lucille is proofreading Jimothy's work. "Were you able to visit Alfred Irving? It would sure be nice to get a quote from the last freed slave in the U.S.", she says. "We must get his testimony. "He was very hard to find. People wouldn't tell me anything", says Jimothy. Lucille sits up drinking her coffee. "They didn't trust reporters?", she asked. "I don't know, I tried sweety". She scoots in close to Jimothy. "Whatever happened to you during the war, we will get through it together", she says. Jimothy kisses her hand. "Don't get started, I have to finish reading your article", she says. Jimothy removes his shirt. "How about we just assume it's perfect and I will…He leans in and whispers in her ear. Lucille puts down the papers and then grabs his hand and leads him to the room.

Ocoee, Florida

Regan and Gator assemble in the kitchen to talk about the future of Ocoee. "My girl Rebecca, who is grown now, thinks white people are the problem. The problem in America has always been the savage Negroes. We need to stop telling them about this history when they turn 16. You're making whites look bad. Mr. Upshaw responds, "we teach them this history to keep them safe. Those who feel entitled to Ocoee will return one day." The parents of Ocoee talk among each other. Regan sends a signal to Gator. He walks over to Mr. Upshaw. "The coloreds decided to leave, and this town is ours. That Is all the children of Ocoee need to know. Mr. Upshaw becomes afraid. "The Negro children, the descendants know. Its not like we can just erase history", he says. Regan interrupts the conversation. "Leave that part to us", we will make sure nobody ever steps foot in our town, trying to take what's ours. Get word to Paul to come to Ocoee".

Jacksonville, Florida

Jimothy is walking through the North side of town in Jacksonville, Florida. He is approached by a larger and stronger Remy, who had seen combat in World War 2. "Remy, how have you been brother. "I feel like I got my brother back". Remy directs Jimothy to a café. "Let's break bread brother". The two enter the café and take a seat. Jimothy orders for the two. "I found Lucille, or should I say she found me. During the war. We are getting married", says Jimothy. Remy doesn't look happy. "Lucille is with CORE. The Congress of Racial Equality", says Remy. "She was in Chicago, now she is home. Our new home", says Jimothy. Jimothy thinks for a minute. "How do you know she is with CORE?", he asked. "I quietly stood at the back of their meetings. Lucille Washington. She said her and her mother fled Ocoee. I didn't speak to her. I knew it was her. I just hope she doesn't get in my way or talk you into getting in my way", he says. Jimothy becomes confused. "I am lost for words", he says. "CORE are a bunch of integrationist. They think they are Ghandi. You can't integrate with evil brother. They work with white people", says Remy.

The two men leave the café and continue their journey up the road. "I don't understand, stop you from what? Are you saying all white people are evil? Remy reaches into his pocket and hands something to Jimothy. He looks down to see a post card with black babies being used as bait for alligators. "What is this? They're using black babies for gator bait?" "You said you're a reporter now, right? Go to Oakland. Talk to Edward Wade.

Jimothy walks into his home to be greeted by Lucille. "Why do you look like you just saw a ghost", she asked. He hands her the postcard. "Babies and alligators", she asked. He points down at the card. "I just saw Remy. He says you're with CORE and he is going in the opposite direction. He wants all out war with whites". She rubs Jimothy's shoulder. "I stand for peace. I stand with CORE. "I have to go", says

Jimothy. He begins to pack a bag. "He saw you and never said a word to you. I don't know what Remy is capable of", says Jimothy. "I will come with you. You need a reporter with experience", says Lucille. The two pack their things and head to Oakland, Florida.

Ocoee, Florida

Regan waits for Wallace to enter the home as she sits at the table and drinks whiskey. He enters the home. "Where is Tim and why are you sitting here drinking in the day?", he asked. "I sent Tim to visit his uncle", she responds. She places a slice of apple pie on the table for her husband. "Eat it", she says. He sits his belongings down. "I'm not really hungry dear", says Wallace. Regan pulls out a gun and lays it on the table. "I said eat the pie or are you full from eating her cooking". Wallace looks surprised. He begins eating the pie. "What did you put in the pie Regan. Regan, what did you put in the pie?" he asked. Regan smirks. "Eat all the pie Wallace. That's it, nice and tasty", she taunts him. Wallace finishes the slice of pie. "You never listen to me like other women listen to their husbands! I feel alone!", he yells. Regan talks while waving her gun around. "I'm not like other women Wallace. You knew that when you married me! You two timing dog". Wallace places the fork down and looks up at his scary wife. "What's in that pie Regan, what's in the pie". She stands up. "Ingredients", she says. Regan continues, "don't you ever cheat on me again. I will bury your Yankee white ass under this house, do you hear me?" Wallace shakes his head as he gets up from the dinner table. She grabs his dish and washes it as he walks away stunned but relieved. "Jesus Christ", he says.

Lucille and Jimothy arrive in Oakland, Florida. They're met by a man named Eddie Wade. "I've heard of traveling light, but you two sure traveled light. Come on, welcome to Oakland and Winter Garden. I want to show you something. The three travelled over to Winter Garden, which is right next to Oakland, which was a very small town. They go into a small store, owned by a white man. "This is Eugene. Eugene, I want you to meet Lucille and Jimothy". Eugene walks over to greet the two. "You two are here for the Gator Bait Post Cards?" Jimothy nods his head. Eugene pulls out a box of them. "My father was a very prejudice man. He hated your people, and he made no apologies". Jimothy asked, "what about you?", as his anger grew. Eugene hands him over a box of post cards. They depict small black babies being used as alligator bait. "This is some kind of satire, right?", asked Lucille. Eugene pushed the drawer closed and directed the three to come with him.

Eugene, Eddie, Lucille and Jimothy all visited a swampy area a little further south. Eugene pulls out a wallet made from alligator skin. "My father made a fortune from gator belts, boots and wallets. People love to buy belts made from the biggest and roughest gators in Florida". Jimothy looks over at the water. "Eugene continues. My pops would tie a rope around a little negro babies' torso. He would place them in the water and then the baby would be swallowed whole by the gator. He would take a club and bash the gator on top of the head. Sometimes the babies died". Lucille almost has a breakdown. "It's true, they used black babies as alligator bait", she says. Eugene continues, "my father did not view your kind as human. I am wealthy because of the sins of my father". They see a gators eyes from a distance in the swampy waters. "Are any white folks using black babies as gator bait now?", asked Jimothy. Eugene pauses. "There is one family. The most feared family in the state of Florida. In order to keep residents from trying to vote, he threatens them, but I don't think he actually takes their babies. His family is well off from selling Gator belts and boots. Eddie Wade looks over at the couple. "Tell them his name, says Eddie. "The Clouds family. Gator Clouds and his brothers have one sister". Eddie Wade pulls more information from Eugene. "Tell them where they live". Jimothy beats them to the punch. "Ocoee and Orlando". Eugene nods his head. "Another fella came through here asking about these post cards months ago". Lucille and Jimothy look at each other. "We have to go", says Jimothy.

Eddie Wade drops the two back off at their car. "I would write about the post cards if I were you. The world should know. Don't pick at fight with the Florida Ku Klux Klan. Your chances of fighting them and surviving are low. I can see it in your eyes. You're ready for war, she isn't", says Eddie. He shakes the couple's hand and then leaves. "Take a breath, we can write about this and make sure we get support on the issue", says Lucille. "Report", he says. Jimothy looks at Lucille with rage in his eyes. "What's wrong?", she asked. "I think it's time somebody got rid of this Gator guy. These people are encouraging our death", Jimothy says. "What good can one man do? We can spread the word. Going to Ocoee or Clearwater or any of these curfew towns is setting yourself up to die", says Lucille. Jimothy opens her car door. "I want to ride home in peace and silence", he says. Lucille looks at Jimothy. He refuses to look her in the eye. Lucille is heartbroken. "I guess I will be silent", she says.

Ocoee, Florida

Regan's daughter Rebecca comes home to visit from college. She hugs her brother Tim and kisses him on the forehead. Regan appears from her room. "Well, if it isn't my daughter, coming back to visit from a college with a bunch of Republican ideas". Rebecca steps back and has a look at her mother. "You don't look well. What is going on mom". Regan looks over at her son. "Can you not make comments like that in front of your brother?", she says. Wallace enters the home to greet his daughter. "You're way in Missouri, where its nice and cold. Are you getting good grades?", he asked. "Father, I am doing well. I am thinking about becoming a lawyer and helping with integration efforts". Regan makes a sound of disapproval. "America will never force the races to mix. Are you doing this to get back at your momma?", asked Regan. "I am doing this to make America a democracy", says Rebecca. "Are you going to talk some sense into your daughter?", Regan asked Wallace. Wallace sighs. "I think what she is doing is brave", he says. Regan stands up. "How dare you go against me!", she yells. "Enough!", Wallace says as he grabs ands shakes his wife. "I am still the man of this house. She doesn't want to grow up to be a hillbilly like you!" Regans mouth drops open. She backs away from her husband. She grabs her whiskey and storms out of the house. Wallace looks at his two kids. "I'm sorry children. I should have never talked to your mom that way".

Gator Clouds is closing one of his stores when he is approached by two men. "Gator, we have come to purchase the remaining Gator Bait post cards you sell. I took up a collection from the people. You will no longer sell this filth of our children being used as bait". Gator turns to face Remy. "Where do I know you from?", asked Gator. The other man steps up to Gator. "It doesn't matter where you know us from. Sell us those post cards now!", the man says. "I don't sell to niggers. You look like niggers to me. You smell like niggers to me, and you sound like niggers to me", he says. "We have money", says Remy. Apparently, you also have a hearing problem", says Gator.

Gator charges at Remy. Remy throws a punch, making Gator step back and spit out his blood. "Oh yeah, I love a nigger who fights back", Gator says. Gator hits the man Remy came with and knocks him out with one blow. Remy steps back and takes a defensive stance as Gator lets out his hardy laugh. Gator charges Remy full speed and tackles him. He begins to choke Remy. Remy reaches a knife on his belt and then cuts Gator from mouth to cheek. Gator lets him go as he begins to bleed from his mouth. One of Gators family members was pulling up to check on Gator as he closed the store. He sees the commotion and shoots Remy's friend as he stands from getting knocked out. Remy runs for it and gets in his car then speeds off as the man shoots at the car. He passes Gator a shirt to hold pressed against his wound. "Don't try to talk, we need to get you to a doctor.

Regan shows at the Doctors office to check on her brother. They had stitched his face. Regan hugs her brother. "Those animals tried to kill you", she says. The doctor hands him something to look at his reflection. Gator stands up. "Gather the boys", he says.

The Ku Klux Klan rides around Florida at night, looking for any black residents that may be alone in Jacksonville, Clearwater and Apopka. Two Klan members spot a man walking home alone after work near Clearwater, Florida. They grab the man and place him in the car. The next morning, residents near by see the man hanging from a tree.

Chapter Six

FREE TO LOVE

Jimothy picks up a newspaper and reads that there is an upswing in lynchings around Florida. A young lady with braided hair is reading the same paper when their eyes meet. "They just keep killing our people", she says. Jimothy nods in agreement. "My name is Sheba", she says. "Your parents named you that?", he asked. "I named me that", she says. Jimothy looks down. "It was nice to meet you", he says as he walks away. The two turn and look at each other.

After sleeping with Sheba, Jimothy stays in her motel room with her. The two lay in bed relaxing. "I am having my last bit of fun and then it is off to Detroit for me. I am seeking the guidance of the Honorable Elijah Muhammad", she says. "You are a Muslim?", Jimothy asked. Sheba sits up on the bed. "I will only be able to marry a Muslim man. Why are you not married? You are a handsome man?", asked Sheba. "I was just about to jump the broom. I called it off", Jimothy replies. "What did she do?", asked Sheba. "My former woman wants peace, and I can't find peace here. Your introduction was they keep killing our people. Where Is the peace in that? I'm too angry inside for her". Sheba rubs on Jimothy's leg. "I would be fighting side by side with you, if you were my husband", she says. Jimothy replies, "I have always hated violence, but I think white people are going to force our hand", he says. Jimothy stands up and then grabs his clothing and gets dressed. "I don't want to worry about love when the war comes", says Jimothy.

Jimothy returns home and gets ready to unlock his door when Lucille appears. "I came to get the rest of my things. She spots a woman's hair on his clothing. she pulls the hair off his shirt. "You moved on pretty fast. It makes me wonder if you ever loved me". "I have never loved anyone but you", Jimothy replies. "How can you disrespect me by laying with another woman? I can smell her scent on you", says Lucille with anger in her voice. She continues, "You're not the man I thought you were". Jimothy replies, "I don't know who I am anymore. You expected me to marry you?" Lucille grabs the rest of her belongings and leave the home the two had shared.

Orlando, Florida

Paul Chumpsky steps off a bus in Orlando, Florida and looks around. He immediately starts putting together meetings and town halls to spread his propaganda. "In America, we have a Negro problem. They keep claiming they are oppressed, but segregation is a blessing. The inferior race and inferior culture should not mix into our culture. Slavery ended almost a century ago and yet they still complain and cry. If these Negros would simply pull themselves up by their bootstraps, then all their problems would be solved. They are a lazy group of people. I say segregation forever!" Crowds cheer and yell "right on brother" at his propaganda.

The Klan march through Sanford, Florida, which is nearby Orlando. A little girl holds on to her mother tight as she looks on at the Klan. The Klan member looks at the young girl from behind his robe. When night falls, they light a cross in the front yard of a residence. The family looks outside an sees the cross burning and then run back in the house. "You niggers live too close to Sanford! Get your black asses back to Orlando!", yells one of the members.

A young man by the name of Jones had been under the teachings of Gator. He decides to travel to Jacksonville, Florida to deliver a message to the people. He sits outside of a popular black-owned café. With his hand shaking, he pulls out a bottle with a rag tucked inside. He steps out of the car and looks around the neighborhood in disgust. He lights the rag on fire and gets ready to toss it when he is shot several times by rifles from a distance. He hears voices from beyond the darkness. He can hear black men yelling, "We burn, you burn, we all burn!" The Klansman drops the bottle and sets himself on fire as he lies dead. Remy and his group had grown tired of the Klan and decided to fight back.

Lucille arrives on the scene the next day to report on the death of the Klansman. White reporters are also on the scene. One of the reporters walk towards her and asked, "do you think this is terrorism by the black community?" Lucille gives the woman a crazy look. "Do you really want to talk about terrorism?", she yells back at the reporter. She looks down at the burned body of the Klansman and then walks away.

Ocoee, Florida

Rebecca left and went back to Missouri. The home was quiet. Tim being an older teenager, he was out chasing girls or hunting most of the time. Regan walks up to Wallace and gives him a hug. "I was thinking with the nest almost empty; we can take time out and love one another again. We can find that love that has been missing". Wallace stands and gives her a kiss on the cheeks. "We come from two different worlds", he responds. Regans tone changed. "You married a country girl like me and now you're standing in judgement of me?", she asked. Wallace attempts to calm her down. "Where do you get the right?", she says. Wallace begins to move away from her. "I should have never moved to the south. The constant hating of Negroes and northerners, it has changed you over the years. You're drinking yourself into an early grave. Look at you", he says. "No, dealing with abusive men like you is what ruined me", she yells back. Wallace goes into the bedroom and starts packing. She blocks the door. "You're not leaving me; I thought I made myself clear. You may not love me or respect me, but you will honor your vowels to me!", Regan says in a rage. Wallce removes her from the doorway. "You will have to shoot me in the back", he says. To his surprise Wallace successfully reaches the door. Gator is standing outside of the door alone in the dark. "Are you going somewhere, Yankee?", he says. Wallace begins to stutter and tries to explain himself. "I know, Yep, I know", says Gator. Regan appears behind Wallace. "I told you, if you ever tried to leave me, I would bury you under this dead coon's house. You brought this on yourself. Never bite the hand that feeds you". Gator strikes Wallace and everything goes black. Regan cries for a moment, but the crying comes to a complete stop. "Did you bring shovels?", she asked Gator. He nods his head.

Orlando, Florida

Lucille returned to Orlando, Florida where she threw herself into her work. A female co worker stops to ask her out to lunch. "You work all day, you need to get something to eat", the woman says. Lucille replies without looking up to acknowledge her. "I will eat when I am ready, thank you". The women quickly walk away from Lucille's office. The woman walks by one of the male reporters. "I don't know what's wrong with her, but she never leaves that office", the woman says to him. "Do you know who that is?", he replies.

The male reporter peeks into her office. "Did you call for me boss?", he asked. "Yes", Lucille says. She holds up his work and continues to speak. "This is 90 percent opinion and 10 percent fact", she says. "Well, President Roosevelt was a Democrat, so I figured why not lean their way", he explained. "If you lean too far, you fall", says Lucille. She hands his work back to him. He walks away as fast as he can.

ACT *Three*

Chapter Seven

THE SECRET OF JULY PERRY

A group called CORE or Congress of Racial Equality begin to stage sit ins and bus rides to demonstrate racial quality through peace. They specialized in teaching the protesters nonviolent tactics such as praying, chanting and singing, or sitting at lunch counters and refusing to get up. CORE had begun to draw criticism from Remy due to their group having mostly white members and refusing to defend themselves when attacked. Remy enters a building where CORE is meeting. "Hey, if your black members are tired of being cowards and running. Come join the real revolution. In the words of the honorable Marcus Garvey, "if they lynch us here, we lynch them in Africa". One of the members stands up and leaves with Remy. They try to get him to stay. The man blurts out, "no, I am tired of being a coward. It's time to fight back! Remy walks out.

Washington D.C.

Jimothy is working on his article, T*hen the Earth Swallowed them Whole*, about the alligator bait postcards circulating in Florida. A young lady named Mabel is lying next to him while he goes through his notes. She proofreads some of it for him. "Are you going for an Ida B. Wells. *Red Record* type of feel?", she asked. "What do you think?", he asked. "I think what kind of sick people would feed babies of any color to an alligator. I also think you need more proof", says Mabel. "I have a post card, what more do I need?", asked Jimothy. "You need a confession, from the store owner, on the record", she responds. Jimothy sits up. "I'm supposed to go back home to Florida, where the Klan is killing folks and get a confession from a white man?", says Jimothy. Mabel kisses him on the cheek. She stands up and puts her skirt on as Jimothy looks up at her curvy frame. "If I had a smart woman like you, then…" She interrupts Jimothy. "You had a smart woman. Go get her back". She gives Jimothy a hug and then heads for the door. "I guess I am going back to Florida", he says.

Ocoee, Florida

Paul sits at the dinner table with Gator and his sister Regan. "It's not enough for me to get out there and talk about how bad the colored folks are. We need to keep showing the world how dangerous they are. As far as these postcards, I don't know, maybe we say they are just a joke". "A joke", Regan says. "You must make people understand how despicable a group is first before you wipe them all out, or else you will get backlash. "Talk about how they cut your face for no reason", says Paul. Hitler learned everything from us". Gator responds, "Hitler loss". "Hitler fought on the wrong side", says Paul.

Orlando, Florida

Jimothy is escorted to the office of Lucille, who was now an editor and a well-known writer. She looks up and sees Jimothy. "Have you come to break my silence", she says. Jimothy looks a little nervous. "This is the first time you have ever not been able to find your tongue", she says. "I need you", says Jimothy. Behind her anger, she feels happy to be needed. "What do you need?", she asked. "A confession from Eugene about what the dad told him regarding the gator bait post cards. If we get a confession, we can more than likely blow this whole thing open", says

Jimothy. "You think a white man is going to go on the record and say that? The Klan would be at his house in a day", she says. "You're better at getting people to talk", he says. She thinks about it for a moment. "My asking price, my name on the story with yours and you never speak to me again. I want to be free to find love and live the rest of my life. You're no good for me", she says. Jimothy shakes his head. "You must really hate me", he says.

Winter Garden, Florida

Eddie Wade takes Lucille and Jimothy back to the store in Winter Garden. Eugene greets the two when they walk in. "You two know you have to be back in Oakland and on your way to Orlando by the time the sun is gone right?", he says. Lucille has a look around the store. "You're such a brave man to help us. God will surely look kindly on you helping with our story", she says. "I won't talk to the press on the record", he says. Jimothy becomes upset. "You're scared your own kind will eat you for dinner aren't you". Lucille holds her hand up to stop Jimothy from escalating the situation out of anger. "You can't say anything on record, but you can leave us some breadcrumbs, can't you?", asked Lucille. "Don't make me look bad Eugene. The Wade family have been buying from you for years", says Eddie. Eugene nods his head. "Come", he says. He shows them gator bait pictures, mugs, and post cards. They depict little babies being used as bait for alligators. He hands him a copy of the Oakland Tribune from 1923, which states "pickaninny bait lures voracious gator to death". Jimothy looks down at the newspaper. "Now Mr. Eugene, I know you're going allow us to walk out of here with this newspaper", she says. "Take it all, most white collectors aren't going to sell. These are very valuable in certain groups of people.

As Jimothy and Lucille walk out of the door, they stop and ask one more question. "If this newspaper was published in 1923, why didn't the government investigate?", asked Jimothy. "You two are from Ocoee right, before the great purge?", asked Eugene. "We are from Ocoee, yes, black folks got ran out of Ocoee", says Jimothy. Eugene pulls a black top hat out. "I won this from a man who was there. He took it from Ocoee Lodge 66, a Negro Masonic Lodge", says Eugene. Jimothy takes the hat. "There was a guy named July Perry". (Lucille and Jimothy give each other a look) "Eugene continues, "well, he was getting ready to empower black people to vote when they killed him. Look closer, you will see that government will never protect black people. The constitution is an inside joke made available to whites". Eugene hands them the top hat. "Don't come back", he says. Eddie Wade nods at Eugene and they exit the store.

Eddie drops Lucille and Jimothy back off at their car in Oakland, Florida. The two look at each other. "The story has become bigger than black children being used as bait. Our own government is unconstitutional", says Lucille. " If we break this story open, it could change America", says Jimothy.

Babies Used as Alligator Bait In State of Florida

The National Association for the Advancement of Colored People, 69 Fifth Avenue, New York, today made public the contents of a dispatch printed in the Louisville, Kentucky, Herald, of September 23, stating that colored babies were being used as alligator bait in the vicinity of Chipley, Florida.

The colored babies are allowed to play in shallow water, with expert riflemen concealed nearby. When the alligator approaches his prey he is said to be shot by the riflemen. The dispatch states that "Florida alligator hunters do not ever miss their tagets. The price reported as being paid colored mothers for the use of their babies as alligator bait, is said to be two dollars.

NEGRO MIGRATION
TO BRING CHANGES
IN ZONING OF CITY

Negro migration from farms to Atlanta has resulted in encroach-

FIVE NEGROES INVOLVED IN STOKES CASE

Chicago, Ill., Oct. 6.—The Cook County Grand Jury on yesterday returned indictments against five Negroes for their alleged part in obtaining evidence for W. E. D. Stokes, wealthy New York hotel owner, upon which to base his suit for divorce from Mrs. Helen Elwood Stokes. Mr. Stokes himself and Daniel Nugent, his attorney of record, were also indicted.

The Negroes under indictment are Robert H. Lee, formerly a Cook County deputy sheriff; Joe Brunner, a cab driver, who is alleged to have distributed large sums of money in obtaining affidavits for Stokes Frank Hubert, formerly head waiter at the Beaux Arts Cafe, who testified that he saw Mrs. Stokes there with a colored man; Mrs. Hattie Johnson, an alleged courier between Stokes and former inmates of the Everleigh

Atlanta Independent Article,
Originally in Oakland Tribune 1923

Article

Then The Earth Swallowed Them Whole

Written by Jimothy Williams

Lucille Washington

1946

My name is Jimothy Williams. I am currently 34 years old. When I was 8 years old, I witnessed the massacre of Ocoee and I also heard about the horror in Rosewood, Florida. Like most victims, I tried to forget. I felt shame, but the shame is on the United States Government and government at all levels for their unconstitutional practices. Lucille and I have put together a timeline, that shows the evil nature of our own government and country.

We are told that the Emancipation Proclamation ended slavery in most states and the Negro gained his citizenship through the Civil Rights Act of 1866 and then it was ratified in the U.S. Constitution in 1868. Our sources reveal that there was a meeting at the Wormley Hotel in Washington D.C., In 1876, during the infamous Tilden or Blood campaign. It was revealed that the freedom of the Freedmen was traded for the states of Louisiana and Florida. The same year, the verdict in United States V. Cruikshank revealed signaling from the U.S. government, that it was open season on the Freedman. July Perry asked the simple question of how a bunch of Ivy League judges could get the 14th Amendment incorrect. We also have Plessy Vs. Ferguson, which on its face can't be equal if one group can separate from the other. If whites can police blacks but the same is not in reverse, how can it be equal?

The United States V. Cruikshank decision and Plessy V. Ferguson signaled to white mobs, who then attacked and burned down over 50 Black communities including Ocoee, Rosewood, Colfax, Tulsa, East St. Louis, Springfield, Slocum, Elaine and so many more. After the Moore V. Dempsey verdict, Under the Taft Supreme Court, you are going to see a slow drop off in large scale racial massacres and genocide. The courts stopped rubber stamping their genocide and they found other ways of using the Ku Klux Klan.

Finally, we have Circular 3591 from the U.S. Justice Department, which reveals that government knew that Black Citizens were still being enslaved and the only reason they ended the practice was out of fear that the Japanese would reveal to the world the hypocrites that are the United States. By bouncing back and forth between the term's peonage, slavery and servitude, but only Black Americans ended up in shackles. This is an old practice going back to the Virginia House of Burgesses who lowered Black people who came to America under a system of Serfdom into permanent chattel slaves.

This government has violated the first Amendment, Second Amendment, 13th Amendment, 14th Amendment and 15th Amendment of Black American Citizens who are Descendants of Freedmen. We provided this information gladly and freely to the public in order to decide what must be done to put an end to the repeated violations of our rights. I believe the United States Government should keep their promise of 40 acres, a order signed by Edwin Stanton.

To white America, whether Republican or Dixiecrat. A government that can turn constitutional rights off and on, may decide to do so to you one day, similar to the Japanese. If you allow it for us, then you allow it for your future generations. This is a calling for the United States to become a Constitutional country that follows the U.S. Constitution forever. God Bless you all.

Chapter Eight

THEN THE EARTH SWALLOWED THEM WHOLE

Jacksonville, Florida

Remy reads the article that was being circulated in academic circles. He had developed the Freedmen's Defense Ministry or the FDM, which had become feared in the south for their will to fight back against the Klan. Jimothy enters the small office to seek out help from his old friend. "Tallboy, what brings you here", says Remy. "Thanks for seeing me. The Freedman's Defense Ministry is growing in power, and I would like your help getting my article to the people. The problem is only the academics are paying attention. "You mean only the uppity Negroes care about your uppity Negro writing?", asked Remy with a smirk. Jimothy holds out his article for Remy to read. "I read it. It was good. But what good is pointing out the wrong of a people who know they are wrong?", asked Remy. He leans forward to whisper to Jimothy. "These crackers don't care". Jimothy responds with, "what's your solution, other than being angry"? Remy stands up. "You never saw any action in the second Great War. I did. I was trapped behind enemy lines, while on a special mission. Most of my team died. I'm not a coward like you. I want war!", says Remy as he bangs his right arm on his chest. "I'm trying to bring awareness", says Jimothy.

Remy gets closer to Jimothy. "Yeah, I know all you do is chase women. You wrote that article with "Ghandi girl", in the end she is going to get you both killed. "You watch your mouth about her", warns Jimothy. Remy shoves him. Jimothy strikes Remy in the chin hard, causing him to fly across the room. Remy gets up and looks at his blood from biting his lip. "I'm proud of you boy. Tallboy got a mean punch. Too bad I have to kill you now". Jimothy turns to see two armed men at the door. One of the men points a revolver at Jimothy. The situation turns tense. Jimothy prepares his mind for death. "Give him the gun", says Remy to his soldier, who now looks confused. "You want to let him go?", says Brutus. Remy signals for his men to give Jimothy the gun. He hands it to him. "Take your misguided anger and get ready for the war to come, because I am bringing it. Next time, you see me, be prepared to kill me", says Remy. Jimothy takes the weapon and walks out of the office before they change their mind.

One of Remy's men speaks. "Boss, we have Klan activity in Clearwater, Sandford and Ocoee. We can go wherever you want. Remy replies, "I want to protect the Negro citizens in Florida. We are putting an end to curfew towns. If were not committing crimes, we should be able to move around this country freely, just like whites. Let the new people know, we are not CORE. If they put their hand on us, we fight back". The Freedman's Defense Ministry had grown since its conception, and they decided to challenge Sundown towns by going where they wanted to.

Gator Clouds visits the home of his sister, Regan. He finds the door cracked so he opens it and walks right in. Regan is giving comfort to a young lady, whose husband had beaten her and given her a black eye. "He's always drunk, he hit me and now I don't even know where he is", says Marge. They look up and see Gator standing in the home. "That little chicken neck Henry beat on her again?", asked Gator. Regan thinks for a moment as she dries the young girls' eyes. "Is he coming back this time?", she asked. "He packed his things. He took his clothes", says Marge. She continues, "I will tell everybody what a two timing, yellow dog he is", she yells. Regan pauses. "Sweetheart, you just saved the South", she says. The woman looks up at Regan in confusion. "You're going to say a nigger raped you. "Do you hear me girl?", says Regan. Marge stands up. "No, I won't be any good to a white man once I say a nigger touched me", she says. "That noodle neck husband of yours ain't around to feed you and you got a hostile womb. You will do as I say, and I will take care of you". The young girl looks up at Gator. He looks down in shame. Regan steps outside and starts yelling for help. "She got raped by a big nigger! Please help. Someone raises the Sheriff. A nigger is on the loose in Ocoee!", says Regan. Regan tries to touch her brother Gators shoulder for support. He was visibly upset and shrugged her off. He walks off.

A white mob begins to form and start snatching black men out of their cars in Apopka and hitting them. Gator approaches one of the men. "I didn't cross the line, Gator! I been doing right!", yells the man. "The thing about a war is only one side can win", says Gator. He stabs the man in the stomach, the man drops to the ground with a look of confusion as he bleeds out. Gator cleans the man's blood off on his pants. He gets in his car and looks for any other black men they can spot.

The Freedman's Defense Ministry arrives in Sanford, Florida. A young man walks up to Remy and whispers something in his ear. "What town are they saying this white girl was raped in", asked Remy. "The young man looks him in the eyes and says, "Ocoee". "How is that even possible? black folk run the other way when they see Ocoee", says Brutus. "It don't need to be true. Ida B. Wells showed us that. They only need to say it and 100 men could die tonight in Florida". Brutus starts to unpack their weapons.

"I say we go to Apopka City and protect the Negro population", says Brutus. Remy nods his head.

Remy and his men drive in two cars toward Apopka but are stopped by a local Sheriff before they could reach the city limit. The Sheriff does not get out of the car. He waits for Gator to join him.

Two more cars pulled up to assist the Sheriff. Brutus sees Gator get out of one of the cars. "That's Gator!", yells Brutus. Gator and his men start shooting up the car of Remy and his men. The two men trailing Remy's car die immediately. Brutus opens his door and steps out. Remy yells "wait", but it was too late. They had shot Brutus as well. Brutus leans against the car bleeding. He manages to lift his shotgun and fire back at the men, killing two of them. The Shotgun pellets tear through the car door as the other men duck for cover. Gator delivers the final shot to the head of Brutus. Remy watches in horror as Brutus goes down. Gator surveys the cars to see if anyone else is alive. He spots Remy moving in the passenger seat. He shoots Remy in the back. Gator gets closer to check the body. As he rolls Remy over, he is surprised to see the black man who had ruined his face. It was a face that Gator would never forget. "You!", says Gator as Remy shoots Gator in the stomach with the gun he was hiding. Gators men get excited and start shooting. Gator tries to step way from Remy and accidently steps on the dark road where he is hit by a fast-moving car. The car stops and a white male gets out to check on Gator. He see's the dead black men. Before the driver could look back up, one of Gators men shoots him in the head. They check to make sure Remy is dead and then put Gators damaged body into the vehicle and drives it back towards Ocoee.

The men pull up to Regan's home and bangs on the door. She comes out to see her brother's body lifeless. "How could you let him die!", yells Regan. She looks down in disbelief. "They killed my brother. The savage animals. They're going to pay. We need to drive over there and kill them all. Randy, one of Gators men walks up and slaps Regan in the mouth. She stands in surprise. "You got Gator killed with your lies. I ain't working for no woman", he says. The rest of the men walk off instead of helping Regan. She starts to scream at the men. "Hey! He hit me. You're going to just let him hit me?". The crowd of onlookers begin to walk away. "Hey!", Regan yells again. She sits in the dirt next to her brother's dead body. Tim comes outside and see's his uncle dead.

Jacksonville, Florida

Jimothy gets news of Remy's death near Ocoee. They also let him know that Gator was killed as well. "They killed my friend", says Jimothy. Jimothy begins to pack his belongings to head for Apopka. Lucille walks up to him as he begins to pack. "You're not even going to discuss this with me. You just pack your bag", she asked. "There is no time. We are out of time my love", says Jimothy. "You're picking revenge over us", she says. "Dammit, some kid is going to die tonight, or watch his family die. I have to be the hero that I needed when I was that kid. That kid was me!", yells Jimothy. Lucille hugs him. "You can't go back and save Tallboy. Let that part of you go", she says. Jimothy goes into his closet and pulls an M1 military rifle. Lucille begins to panic. "I can't build a life with someone who is unstable as you!", she says. "My life belongs to the people", Jimothy responds. "The people get you and I get your dead body to bury", she says. Jimothy continues to pack. Lucille grabs a few of her things. "I am going with you", she says. He shakes his head. "I am a grown woman. I can find a ride, or you can take me with you", she demands. Against his better judgement, Jimothy agrees and the two hit the road.

Paul gathers in a town hall of Florida residents after several members of their beloved Ku Klux Klan was killed. Today, I have the Daughters of the Confederacy with me. They have passed down the story of how the Yankees blamed us for slavery and then started a war of northern aggression against us. The women one by one talk about how their grandfathers were killed in action during the civil war. "The elite Republicans and their criminal-colored people took over our town in South Carolina", says one of the women. "We gave the Africans Christianity, and they turned on us", said another woman. The women go on about how peaceful things were until the Yankees from the north made slavery an issue and how slavery was exaggerated.

Paul stands. "From this day forward, we control the history that will be taught to our young people. No more colored people pretending to be victims of the bad white people. Any books or articles that mention Ocoee or Rosewood must be banned. We do not want the Yankee to keep teaching our kids these lies. The Japs attacked us first and they got what they deserved. The niggers can't survive without us. It ain't our fault God didn't make them with intelligence. We were taking care of them. How do you turn your back on people who make sure you have food? Look at the Negro now, they can barely survive without us. The Republicans should no longer interfere with our affairs, agreed upon in 1876. It is time for the nigger problem to go away for good". People stand up and cheer Paul.

Mr. Upshaw drives Tim back home after seeing Paul speak. "Listen, I'm sorry about your uncle. He was a fine man. I go back a way with your family. He drops Tim off at his home and knocks on the door. Tim just goes into the house. They find the body of Regan at the table dead. Her whiskey flask had fell out of her hand and on to the floor. Mr. Upshaw tries to grab Tim and guide him out of the home, but he turns and looks at his mother's body. "They killed my uncle and now they killed my mother. I bet they also killed my dad!". "Who?", asked Mr. Upshaw. "You know who. Those animals. They're animals and they should be in cages!", yells Tim. Mr. Upshaw grabs Tim and slaps him. "Let me slap the stupid out of you right now boy! I don't want you to end up like your uncle or your mother. Listen, they had good hearts, but your family are part of the damn problem. You can't let your hate for them stop you from living your life. You are going to pack your things and I'll take you off to college like your sister. You must get far away from this place. There is nothing here for you. I told Gator, Jerry, to settle down with a Christian woman and live his life years ago. You better go live your life my boy". Tim breaks down crying. Mr. Upshaw guides him to get the rest of his stuff so that he can take him away from his mother's body. "As far as your father, he probably ran away. But learn from him what not to do! Real men stick around!", says Mr. Upshaw.

Rebecca receives word at school in Missouri that her mother and uncle had passed away. She worked on a paper called the History we Lost. The report states, "I don't know why we hate the Negro or why they hate us. I just know my family raised me that way. There are many people who want the history of Ocoee and Rosewood gone forever. I found other massacres all across America. These people's businesses were burned down. These people's homes were taken or burned down. The Colfax Massacre, which kicked it all off. The Massacre in Louisiana which helped the 14th Amendment get passed. We often say the Negro should just get over slavery, but perhaps it is us who have not gotten over it. My uncle just passed away. He caused death and pain to other families. He ran my father off. Those children are just kids just like ours and the thought that people would use them for gator bait or even suggest it on post cards to collect is sick in itself".

As students read her paper, that was being circulated all over the school, one student looks at another and says, "she is teaching whites to feel guilty and hate ourselves. We haven't done anything wrong. The other girl says, "this is just politics". The two girls throw the paper on the floor and walk off. Rebecca packs her bags and looks at her dorm before leaving to bury her uncle. Young girls from Missouri stare at her in anger after reading her paper. One of the girls "yells traitor. Nigger lover", as Rebecca looks back. The dorm director guides her to her ride. She leaves campus and later attends Yale Law School. A school that her uncle hated because Jewish people were allowed to attend.

Winter Garden, Florida

Eddie Wade helps Eugene pack up his shop. He sold it and decided to retire. "What are you going to do when you leave Florida?", asked Eddie. "I guess whatever I want. You be safe Eddie. I pray that your family is safe", says Eugene. He sticks out his white hand and Eddie shakes it. "Safe travels to you, old man", says Eddie. Eddie watches Eugene drive off and then heads back to Oakland, Florida.

Grease decides to travel the country selling copies of Then the Earth Swallowed them Whole. A report on the Ocoee Massacre, Circular 3591, and the corrupt meeting to trade Florida and South Carolina in an election for the freedom of all Black Americans in 1876. Many of the black residents didn't want to read it and didn't want to be reminded of the events. Grease still goes around selling it to whoever is willing to listen.

Jimothy and Lucille stop near Sandford, Florida, on their way to investigate what happened to Remy. Jimothy helps Lucille grab her belongings to place inside a motel. "When is the last time you heard some good music", asked Jimothy. She hugs him. "Forever", she says. The couple goes into town to get something to eat. Black workers are cleaning up and getting ready to go home before it gets too dark.

Paul is gathered around talking, while others watch. "We are taking the state of Florida back. We are taking Florida back from the Yankees. We are not going to allow them to teach our children to mix with the colored race. God created us to be apart from one another. When CORE comes to Sandford, we will run them out. No more of this communist filth. If the elites and the colored people get their way, they will have their sons marrying your daughters. The crowd begins to grow as Paul speaks.

Jimothy and Lucille wait away from the crowd, watching black workers packing up to go. A lady stops and speaks to them. "You might want to go to Orlando, things have been a little scary around here lately".

A white man yells at Paul from the crowd. "Hey, our niggers clean our homes, and they leave. They haven't been kicking up fuss in Sandford. I remember you. You were causing fuss down there in Clearwater", says the man. Some members of the crowd want Paul to leave and some cheer him on. "Orlando it is", says Jimothy. He guides Lucille to the car. "Paul decides to turn it up a notch". "As far as nigger babies being fed to alligators, I think they make tasty little morsels", says Paul as members of the crowd laugh. One of the workers points and yells, "Jesus don't like people killing no children now! Do you think God is coming back for a segregated church?", she yells. Jimothy had almost reached the car when she said it. He says to himself, "shit". Paul points at the woman and yells, "abomination!" people begin to throw rocks at the black woman for speaking out. A rock hits her in the head.

Lucille runs over to save the woman from the crowd. They hit Lucille with a rock. One of the men in the crowd shoots the car window out of Jimothy's automobile. He runs and uses his body to shield Lucille. He grabs the women and tries to put them in the car, but several men come running after them. Jimothy strikes one of the men and the other turns and runs to go grab his gun. Jimothy signals for a young man to drive his car and get the women out of there. Lucille tries to get Jimothy to come. "No, I'm done running", he says. Lucille repeats his name, but he stops listening. They get ready to drive off when he finally yells, "I love you, now go!". The young man steps on the gas and drives them away. In the commotion Jimothy had grabbed a case and opened it. He pulled out his M1 rifle. Jimothy turns hits a man coming to attack him in the face with the butt of his M1. He spots the other man coming back with a gun. Jimothy takes aim and shoots the man with the M1 killing him. He turns the M1 on a man chasing after a black woman on a horse with a gun and shoots him, causing him to flip off the horse. A man shoots Jimothy and he drops the M1. He was hit in the shoulder and started bleeding. Jimothy falls but grabs the revolver that Remy had given him. He returns fire killing the man who shot him. People are running everywhere. A car pulls up and yells get in to Jimothy. He jumps in the car, and they take off, leaving the M1 behind. A man grabs the M1 and tries to aim at the car but discovers there is no more bullets.

Jimothy is trying to stop the bleeding in the car that picked him up. "Did you see where the boy took the woman I was with". The driver looks back. "No, but you need some medical care. I'm sure she will be in Orlando, but they will be looking for you in Orlando too". Jimothy thinks about all the time he has wasted being apart from his soulmate. If he was going to die, he wanted her to be around.

Lucille reaches Orlando and is walking around hopelessly searching for Jimothy. The woman that was hit in the head with a rock is being looked at by a medical doctor. Lucille checks on her and brings her some water. "Sweety, have you found your husband?", she asked. The woman asked. She almost says he isn't her husband but stops herself. "I can't find him", she says. She rubs on the ladies back to help her feel better.

Washington D.C. 3 months later.

Lucille is in Washington D.C. reporting on how Thurgood Marshall and other attorneys won Morgan V. Virginia. People thought it would be the end of Jim Crow, but many black residents were still too afraid to challenge the police and Southern Governors. She was having lunch with her friend Debra, who had taken a job in Washington D.C. "Do you think Morgan V. Virginia will be the end of Jim Crow? Do you think Thurgood Marshall will be the one, who breaks the back of segregation?", asked Debra. A tall man serves them coffee. They looked up to see that Jimothy had found Lucille. She stands up and hugs him. "How did you find me?", she asked. "I follow your work and I know you love coffee. Grease told me you were in D.C. and living the fancy life", he says. Debra interrupts. "Well, are you staying in D.C. and getting married? Are you going to keep vanishing on my friend?", she asked. Jimothy drops some money on the table to pay for their meal and then he asks for Lucille's hand.

Jimothy takes Lucille to the Lincon Memorial. "I get so busy, I forget that the memorial is even here", she says. Lucille looks over and sees Jimothy holding a wedding ring. She stops talking. "Is that a, yes?", he asked. "It's about time!", she says. Jimothy is so happy he lifts Lucille when he hugs her. Other people looking at the Monument, both black and white, begin to cheer for the couple.

Alligator Bait.

Louisiana

Paul finds himself in Louisiana after causing too much trouble in Florida. He decides to spread his ideas throughout the entire south. He eats at a dinner, but the food was too spicey for him. "Water, please water", he yells. Paul finally relieves himself of the agony from the spicey food. He goes into a poor area In New Orleans and decides to sleep with a black woman. "I must say I am not a big fan of the food here, but I sure love Creo women." The woman guides Paul to her bedroom.

Paul leaves the woman's home after placing money on her nightstand. He practices his next speech with nobody around as he walks down the street. "The Negro race is a hateful race. They are a disgraceful race. You can't trust them, just like we can't trust the Japs. But, not to worry, I have invented the solution to get rid of the Americans Negro problem you see. Paul keeps walking until he see's two white men walking in his direction. "Ah, you look like two decent Christian men. Have I told you about the Negro problem in America?", he asked the men. The two men walk by. One whispers, "This guy is drunk". Paul continues on his aimless walk when the two men double back and take turns stabbing Paul to death. Paul falls on the ground, surprised that a fellow white man could do harm to him. Paul dies in the New Orleans heat. The men reach in his pockets and take his money.

Tim refuses to join his sister and instead walks around Ocoee with a picture of his father, asking if anyone had seen him. Tim was heartbroken but knew his father Wallace would never leave him. Rebecca is still getting a good education at Yale law, she got married and quickly took her husband's name in order to distance herself from her family. Rebecca and her brother had not taken Wallace's name, but instead used Clouds.

Grease is still selling Then the Earth Swallowed them Whole, while telling people walking by that he knows the people wrote it. "Come on down and get your copy! Don't be sloppy, get your copy. My name is Grease baby", he yells.

Flashback 1920

July Perry meets Mr. Hightower in front of Ocoee Lodge Number 66 and hands him a note before going inside. Mr. Hightower opens the note. The brothers at the lodge stand and give a toast to July Perry. He stands and speaks for a moment. "I know you all understand the power that comes with voting, but there is also power in standing up for yourself and saying I am a citizen, and no man will take my rights away. It is on this truth; we fight for future generations. I promise you; this will not last forever".

Mr. Hightower makes it home after closing the lodge. He opens the note. Mr. Hightower reads it and then burns it by candlelight. He calls his wife. "Sweetheart, pack a few things just in case for tomorrow", he says. She nodded in agreement. "What about the Judge, July Perry spoke with Judge Cheney didn't he?", she asked. Mr. Hightower looks up at her. "God is the ultimate judge and the only judge we need", he says. Mr. Hightower says to himself, "alright brother Perry".

After the massacre, Judge Cheney sees the body of July Perry hanging. He packs his things and leaves Orlando.

Flashback within the Flashback
July 25, 1912

President Taft stands to appoint Judge Cheney to the Southern District of Florida as a Federal Judge. Judge Cheney raises his right hand. "I will faithfully discharge my duties and uphold the Constitution of the United States Mr. President. "I know you will", says President Taft. He shakes Judge Cheney's hand as he looks up at the large President.

Forward to 1923

Judge Taft calls his law clerk to his office. "Issue a Writ of Certiorari for Moore v. Dempsey and bring everything you have", he asked. The clerk comes back with a file and hands it to Judge Taft. "Did Judge Cheney ever speak to you after the lynchings in Ocoee", asked the clerk. Judge Taft doesn't respond, he just looks down at the file. "Thank you", he says to the clerk.

The End

Story and Soundtrack Written by E.J. Wade

Source code

Oakland Tribune. Babies Used as Alligator Bait in the State of Florida. 1923. Reprint. Atlanta Independent

E.J. Wade. 2021. Where Jim's Crows go to Die. Formerly known as. The Wormley Agreement: Ghosts of Confederate Soldiers

U.S. Reports Moore V. Dempsey 1923, 261. U.S. 86 1923. Library of Congress

The Little-Known Story of America's Deadliest Election Day Massacre- Ocoee. Smithsonian Magazine. Isis Davis Marks. 2020

United States V. Cruikshank 92 U.S. 542 Library of Congress

Sothern Horrors, Lynch Law and All its Phases. Ida B. Wells 1892

OPPAGA.FL.GOV Ocoee Election Day Violence, November 1920

Circular 3591 Number 19 Supreme Court Docket William L. Burrel Jr. Supreme Court of the United States

PBS. Slavery by Another Name Circular 3591. History Background, NOB Wagner. 2012

In Loving Memory of Julius July Perry
In Loving Memory of Eddie Wade
In Loving Memory of Lillie Mae Wade
In Loving Memory of Ida Bell Wells-Barnett
In Loving Memory of the Victims of the Ocoee Massacre
In Loving Memory of the Victims of the Colfax Massacre

www.ingramcontent.com/pod-product-compliance
Lightning Source LLC
Chambersburg PA
CBHW070825260726
48660CB00005B/1991